ROSS MACDONALD

Scott and Ernest: The Authority of Failure and the Authority of Success
Ernest Hemingway, Cub Reporter (*editor*)
Ernest Hemingway's Apprenticeship (*editor*)
Hemingway at Auction (*editor, with C. E. Frazer Clark, Jr.*)
Raymond Chandler: A Descriptive Bibliography
Chandler Before Marlowe (*editor*)
Ring Lardner: A Descriptive Bibliography (*with Richard Layman*)
Some Champions: Sketches & Fiction by Ring Lardner
(*editor, with Richard Layman*)
The O'Hara Concern: A Biography of John O'Hara
"An Artist Is His Own Fault": John O'Hara on Writers and Writing (*editor*)
John O'Hara: A Descriptive Bibliography
Selected Letters of John O'Hara (*editor*)
Just Representations: A James Gould Cozzens Reader (*editor*)
James Gould Cozzens: New Acquist of True Experience (*editor*)
James Gould Cozzens: A Descriptive Bibliography
James Gould Cozzens: A Life Apart
Kenneth Millar/Ross Macdonald: A Descriptive Bibliography

HBJ ALBUM BIOGRAPHIES

EDITED BY MATTHEW J. BRUCCOLI

ROSS MACDONALD *by Matthew J. Bruccoli*

JACK KEROUAC *by Tom Clark*

JAMES JONES *by George Garrett*

ROSS MACDONALD

BY

MATTHEW J. BRUCCOLI

Harcourt Brace Jovanovich, Publishers   •   San Diego   New York   London

HBJ

Requests for permission to make copies of any part of the work should
be mailed to: Permissions, Harcourt Brace Jovanovich, Publishers,
Orlando, Florida 32887

Selected Letters of Raymond Chandler, copyright © 1981 College
Trustees Ltd. By Permission of Helga Greene.
Excerpts from unpublished manuscripts and letters and the pub-
lished work of Kenneth Millar printed by permission of Harold Ober
Associates Incorporated and the Margaret Millar and Kenneth
Millar 1981 Trusts. Copyright © 1984 by Margaret Millar and Ken-
neth Millar 1981 Trusts.
Excerpts from Blue City (1947), The Three Roads (1948), The Mov-
ing Target (1949), The Drowning Pool (1950), The Barbarous
Coast (1956), The Doomsters (1958), The Galton Case (1959), The
Far Side of the Dollar (1965), Black Money (1966), Archer in
Hollywood (1967), The Instant Enemy (1968), The Goodbye Look
(1969), Archer at Large (1970), The Underground Man (1971),
Introduction to Great Stories of Suspense (1974), The Blue Ham-
mer (1976), Archer in Jeopardy (1979) published by permission of
Alfred A. Knopf, Inc.
Excerpts from Alfred A. Knopf's 2 September 1948 letter to Ken-
neth Millar published by permission of Alfred A. Knopf, Inc. All
rights reserved.
Material from the Alfred A. Knopf Papers used by permission of
Alfred A. Knopf, Inc., and the Humanities Research Center, Uni-
versity of Texas, Austin.
A condensed version of this book originally appeared in Saturday
Night magazine in Canada.

Library of Congress Cataloging in Publication Data
Bruccoli, Matthew Joseph, 1931–
Ross Macdonald.
(HBJ album biographies)
Bibliography: p.
Includes index.
1. Macdonald, Ross, 1915– 1983 .   2. Novelists,
American—20th century—Biography.   I. Title.
II. Series: HBJ album biography series.
PS3525.I486Z6   1983   813'.52 [B]   83–293
ISBN 0–15–179009–4
ISBN 0–15–679082–3 (pbk.)

Designed by Joy Chu
Printed in the United States of America
First edition
A B C D E

In Memory of Roy LaVia, KIA

But time is always guilty. Someone must pay for
Our loss of happiness, our happiness itself.

W. H. Auden, "Detective Story"

. . . to take the psychic event which has occurred
in all of us, the guilty loss of togetherness and
innocence, and put it back into the external world
where it has its repercussions.

Kenneth Millar in a BBC interview

CONTENTS

Contents

❧ FOUR ❧
92

ACKNOWLEDGMENTS

THESE are some of the people and organizations that have helped me:
Ivan von Auw, Jeanne Bennett, William Cagle (Lilly Library, Indiana
University), Barnaby Conrad, Patricia Cork, and Aubrey Davis (Hughes
Massie, Ltd.), Donald Davie, Ellen Dunlap (Humanities Research Center,
University of Texas), Robert Easton, William C. Gault, Ashbel Green (Al-
fred A. Knopf), Herbert Harker, Hugh Kenner, Natalie Kuguenko, Dennis
Lynds, David Monaghan, Mystery Writers of America, Maurice Neville,
Dorothy Olding (Harold Ober Associates), Anthony Rota, R. L. Samsell,
Ralph B. Sipper, Dr. Michael Sribnick, Julian Symons, Stuart Taylor
(*Santa Barbara News-Press*), Willard H. Temple, Eleanor Van Cott (Seed,
Martin & Mackall), Elizabeth Walter (Collins), and Peter Wolfe. Jill Kre-
mentz provided key photographs. I made use of the manuscript collections
at the University of California, Irvine; the Lilly Library, Indiana Uni-
versity; Princeton University; and the University of Texas, Austin.
Heather Barker and Michael Mullen, my research assistants, provided ex-

traordinary aid. Arlyn Bruccoli performed her customary discouraging editorial services. Professor George Geckle, Chairman of the University of South Carolina Department of English, has consistently facilitated my work in every way within his power.

My largest debts are to Margaret Millar; Roger Berry (Curator of Special Collections, University of California, Irvine); and Harriet Oglesbee, Lori Finger, Susan Bradley, and Beth Woodward (Interlibrary Loan Department, Cooper Library, University of South Carolina). Catherine Coleman retyped this book until she was satisfied with it. Judith Baughman's proofreading went beyond proofing.

CHRONOLOGY

13 December 1915   Birth of Kenneth Millar in Los Gatos, California, to John Macdonald Millar and Annie Moyer Millar.

1919   Move to Canada; separation of parents.

1919–1928   Lives with Canadian relatives in several locations.

1928–29?   Attends St. John's School, Winnipeg, Canada.

1930–32   Attends Kitchener-Waterloo Collegiate & Vocational School.

1932   Death of father provides small legacy for college education.

1933	Enters University of Western Ontario.
1935	Death of mother.
1936–37	Travels in Europe.
1938	A.B., University of Western Ontario.
2 June 1938	Marriage to Margaret Ellis Sturm.
1938–39	Graduate courses at Ontario College of Education, University of Toronto.
June 1939	Birth of Linda Jane Millar.
1939–41	Teacher, Kitchener Collegiate Institute.
1941	Publication of Margaret Millar's *The Invisible Worm*.
1941–44	Graduate student, University of Michigan.
1944–46	Ensign, lieutenant j.g., U.S. Naval Reserve. Communications officer aboard escort carrier *Shipley Bay*.
1944	*The Dark Tunnel* (Kenneth Millar).
1946	*Trouble Follows Me*.
March 1946	Moves to Santa Barbara, California.
1947	*Blue City* (first novel published by Knopf).
1948	*The Three Roads*.
1949	*The Moving Target* (John Macdonald). First Lew Archer novel.

1950   *The Drowning Pool* (John Ross Macdonald).

1951   *The Way Some People Die.*

1952   Ph.D., University of Michigan.

1952   *The Ivory Grin.*

1953   *Meet Me at the Morgue.*

1954   *Find a Victim.*

1955   *The Name Is Archer.*

1956   *The Barbarous Coast* (Ross Macdonald).

1956–57 Undergoes psychotherapy, Menlo Park, California.

1958   *The Doomsters.*

1959   *The Galton Case.*

1960   *The Ferguson Affair.*

1961   *The Wycherly Woman.*

1962   *The Zebra-Striped Hearse.*

1964   *The Chill.*

1965   *The Far Side of the Dollar.*

1966   *Black Money.*

1968   *The Instant Enemy.*

1969   *The Goodbye Look.*

1971   *The Underground Man; Newsweek* cover story.

1973   *Sleeping Beauty.*

1974   Grand Master Award, Mystery Writers of America.

1976   *The Blue Hammer.*

1980   Onset of Alzheimer's disease.

11 July 1983   Death of Kenneth Millar in Santa Barbara.

INTRODUCTION

IN "The Guilty Vicarage: Notes on the Detective Story, by an Addict" (1948), an influential apology for reading detective fiction as escapist pleasure, W. H. Auden admitted that for him "detective stories have nothing to do with works of art."[1] He regarded the pure detective story as the murder-in-the-English-countryside mystery in which innocence is violated and then restored.

According to Auden's tests, Raymond Chandler's "serious studies of a criminal milieu" are not detective stories and "should be read and judged, not as escape literature, but as works of art." That endeavor received no further attention from Auden. In what is loosely categorized as the American hard-boiled detective novel, there is no restoration of an Edenic state. (Most of the best American detective novels are set in California, 6,000 miles west of Eden.) The private eye redresses particular wrongs, but disorder—not order—is the underlying condition.

The hard-boiled (sometimes called the tough-guy) novel, which combines elements of romanticism and realism, is America's unique contribution to detective fiction—apart from its formulation by Edgar Allan Poe. Critics have traced the pedigree of the hard-boiled detective to the nineteenth-century English gentleman amateur detective. Although the American private eye and the English gentleman manifest a personal code of honor—a determination to redress the wrongs that the agents of the law are unable to deal with—the crucial difference is that the English amateur is an establishment figure, whereas the American private detective is an outsider as well as a professional. In a corrupt society he stands apart from both the criminal and the cop. He gets paid for what he does, but he does it for its own sake.

Another American who tried for art was Kenneth Millar—a one-time Auden pupil. Like most writers who work seriously with a form that has been categorized as escapist, his road to recognition was long and his arrival was late. This book traces Millar's popular and critical reputations, which developed at different rates. The effort is worth while because he is one of the three American writers of detective fiction—along with Dashiell Hammett and Chandler—who achieved serious critical attention.*

The process is familiar: the gradual accretion of a following among mystery buffs, climaxed by the discovery of Millar's twenty-first novel by the literary opinion makers, followed by a counterassessment. Although all of Millar's novels were initially published in cloth, his reputation was launched from the paperback racks. Millar's case differs from Chandler's and Hammett's in that there was more evidence to go on: seventeen post-apprentice novels between 1949 and 1969. Yet his productivity almost certainly impeded his critical or official recognition. An anti-output bias operates on literary stratification. Productive writers are suspect—in many cases rightly. There is a belief that good books must marinate for years. Hacks are productive by definition, but productivity is not the test of a trivial writer. Millar's novels were carefully written and painstakingly revised. He wrote a great deal because he had to support himself and because he had a great deal to write about.

There is a publishing anecdote about the paperback editor who called in one of his most productive authors and told him, "You're a very good writer, but you're writing too fast. I'm going to give you an advance so that

---

* James M. Cain has been accorded respectful attention, including Millar's; but he wrote crime novels—not detective fiction.

you can take a year off and write a really good book." A year later the writer came back with four novels. One of the lessons of this parable is that writers write the only way they can write.

Outsiders have difficulty comprehending that literature is an occupation, whatever else it may be. Like any other occupation, it must provide a livelihood for the writer. Civilians also seem to assume that any published book makes a lot of money. Arithmetic is instructive. *The Moving Target* (1949), Millar's first Lew Archer novel, sold no more than 5,000 copies in cloth at \$2.50 per copy (10% royalty × \$2.50 × 5,000 = \$1,250). The Mystery Guild reprint probably brought another \$500. The English cloth editions sold 3,124 copies at 10 shillings/6 pence—earning the author perhaps \$500. If the 25-cent Pocket paperback sold 50,000 copies at 1 cent per copy royalty, it brought him \$500. Plus another \$500 for the English paperback. Or \$3,250 for a successful mystery that was selected by a book club and republished in England. Even if these estimates are 50 percent off, the total would be \$4,875 for a year's work—less 10 percent agent's commission and typing fees. *The Moving Target* later brought in a good deal of money when it was made into a movie, but when it was published the author cashed checks totaling something between \$2,925 and \$4,388.

It was fortunate that for Millar the requirements of economics and art overlapped. He wrote for money, but he wrote for the audience he wanted to reach. And given his almost compulsive probing of certain themes, it can be said that he wrote what he had to write.

Critical acclaim and financial reward were sweet when they came; but by that time Kenneth Millar had done his best work.

ROSS MACDONALD

❧❧ ONE ❧❧

I N 1939 the Toronto *Saturday Night* published a short-short story, "The Yellow Dusters," in which a schoolboy living in a furnished room with his mother endures the humiliations of poverty and an institutionalized father. His mother attempts to earn money by peddling dustcloths door to door: "The woman's voice went on and on, planning the impossible, drunken with hope. The agony was twisting the boy's stomach like an iron hand."[1] The author was a twenty-four-year-old Ontario high school teacher who had "committed the sin of poverty"[2] in fifty rooms before he was sixteen.

The spiritual descendant of Oliver Twist and Jay Gatsby, Kenneth Millar was born in Los Gatos, California, in the San Francisco Bay area, on 13 December 1915. His parents were John Macdonald Millar and Annie Moyer Millar. Both forty-year-old Canadians, they had come to California from Great Slave Lake in the Northwest Territories, where he had edited a newspaper and she had organized a nursing station. John was the son of an immigrant Scottish newspaper editor, and Annie was one of seventeen children of a village storekeeper descended from Pennsylvania Dutch farmers. When his only child was born, John wrote celebratory verses published in the *Los Gatos Mail.*

OOR KENNIE

(1)

December's glaur was thick the
   morn
That Jock and Nannie's bairn was
   born.
His name is Kenneth, and you
   ken
That Kenneth's been the name
   of men.
A Celt strain within him flows
Of Chiefs who wore the kilt and
   hose:
Whose foemen oft were wont to
   feel
The keenness of their broad-
   swords' steel:
Who skirled the pipes on Scottish
   braes,
Where winds were cold, and scant
   their claes,
And worshipped with their sword
   in hand
When persecution stalked the
   land.

(2)

Another race of men he claims
Besides the clans with Gaelic
   names.
From where wild torrents rush
   and leap

Through rugged canyons broad
    and deep,
Where peaceful vales in sunshine
    lie,
And Jungfrau summits pierce the
    sky.
These sturdy forbears came away
To Freedom's shores in early day,
From where the enslaver's hosts
    strove long
To drive them with the subject
    throng.

(3)

The Teuton and the Celtic blood,
    The Saxon and the Gaul,
Are intermingled in his veins,
    He lays good claims to all:
And in the melting pot that's made
    This possible to be,
May he, and all mankind, yet find
    Abiding charity.[3]

From Los Gatos the Millars moved to Vancouver, British Columbia, where John supported them as a harbor pilot; but Annie felt that her husband neglected work for his hobbies. He was romantically drawn to the Far West and the Far North, and one of his interests was the folklore of the local Indians and Japanese. When their son was three, John abandoned his family without warning. Kenneth left Vancouver with his mother, taking with him the memory of a trip on a harbor boat with his father. For the next fifteen years he was a charity case, often the unwelcome guest in somebody else's home.

Although Annie was a trained nurse, her health had been broken by typhoid fever, and she was unable to support herself and her son. When Kenneth was six, his mother prepared to place him in an orphanage, taking him as far as the gates before relenting. He never forgot those orphanage gates. Kenneth was taken in by his uncle and aunt, Rob and Beth Millar, on Georgian Bay in Ontario. Rob was the projectionist for the local movie house, where Kenneth fed his dreams on the *Perils of Pauline* and other serials. When he was eleven he read *Oliver Twist* with a thrill of identification. Just as Dickens's Dickensian childhood shaped his own work, Kenneth recognized that literature was a form of wish fulfillment or escape or even revenge: "We never forgive our childhood. What makes a novelist is the inability to forget his childhood."[4]

This relatively happy period ended with the death of Beth Millar when Kenneth was twelve, and he was given a train ticket to Winnipeg, where his Aunt Margaret sent him to St. John's School, a semi-military academy. For two years Kenneth saw how more fortunate boys lived. In Winnipeg he discovered the adventures of Falcon Swift the Monocled Manhunter in the *Boys' Own Magazine*, an English pulp weekly, and began writing western fiction and a long narrative poem about Bonnie Prince Charlie. The 1929 crash terminated his stay at St. John's, and he was passed to his Aunt Laura in Medicine Hat, Alberta. Among the dozen relatives he lived with was "the dangerous one who carried a heavy handgun in his Packard. He may have inspired some of my best work."[5]

The final stop on what seemed Kenneth's odyssey to nowhere was Kitchener, Ontario, sixty miles from Toronto, where he lived with his grandmother and an aunt in an atmosphere of fundamentalist gloom and guilt. "In a puritanical society the poor and fatherless, suffering the quiet punishments of despair, may see themselves as permanently and justifiably damned for crimes they can't remember having committed."[6] In his childhood Kenneth had also seen real crimes committed. "I write about what I know," he later declared.[7] In 1973 Millar responded to the Supreme Court ruling on obscenity by stating, "There are subjects very close to me which I intend to write about. . . . going back into generations of my own family. . . . that seem important for me to write about and since they do have to do with the Puritan experience in Canada, where my family lived, these new rules could make it impossible for me to write honestly about it."[8] Illness terminated his writing before he could openly use this material.

In September 1930 Kenneth entered the Kitchener-Waterloo Collegiate & Vocational School, from which he graduated in 1932. During these years the local library, presided over by B. Mabel Dunham, a published novelist, became the place where he lived outside of school hours

Dashiell Hammett at the Hotel Lombard, January 1934
(Photography Collections, Humanities Research Center, University of Texas)

until he went home to sleep. Some of the authors who excited and influenced him were Dostoevski, Coleridge (he planned to complete "Christabel"), Wilkie Collins, Stephen Leacock—and, probably later, Morley Callaghan, H. L. Mencken, and F. Scott Fitzgerald. In 1979 Millar responded to the question "What book made you decide to become a writer and why?" by naming Leacock. "He brought together the strands of the North American literary tradition, marrying old-world and new-world English, the spoken and the written and the printed."[9]

At this time Kenneth discovered Hammett: ". . . One day in 1930 or 1931 I found *The Maltese Falcon* on a shelf of a lending library in a Kitchener tobacco shop, and I read a good part of it on the spot. It wasn't escape reading. As I stood there absorbing Hammett's novel, the slot machines at the back of the shop were clanking and whirring, and in the billiard room upstairs the perpetual poker game was being played. Like iron filings magnetized by the book in my hands, the secret meanings of the city began to organize themselves around me like a second city."[10] This period of literary stimulation was also a time of anger and desperation because he hated his deprived life and saw no way out: "I was a rebel in most respects; I used to take incredible risks."[11] Millar later admitted that he "narrowly escaped becoming a criminal" and said that his deprived youth provided him with an understanding of how criminals are formed by social exclusion.[12] His academic record was undistinguished—his most frequent grade was C (50 to 59 percent)—but in later years he was proud of the excellent education he had received in Canada. He read and wrote steadily on his own, sometimes consuming a book before breakfast.

At Kitchener-Waterloo Collegiate & Vocational School, Kenneth Millar appeared in print for the first time with "The South Sea Soup Co.," a parody of Arthur Conan Doyle that opens, "The ambitious young investigator, Herlock Sholmes, yawned behind his false mustache and poured for himself a cocaine-and-soda."[13] (The by-line read Ken Miller.) The issue of *The Grumbler* in which he broke into print also published a story about a dying pianist by his fellow debater, Margaret Sturm. Two more appearances followed in *The Grumbler*, "Philo France, in the Zuider Zee" (another detective parody) and "To the Damned Their Due . . ." (a short-short story).

During his Canadian hegira his mother encouraged him to think of himself as an American by virtue of his California birth. California assumed the aspect of a lost kingdom where he would one day reclaim his birthright. If he was not truly a displaced person, Kenneth developed a split viewpoint, a sense of dual citizenship, and—most important for his literary career—a double perspective on two cultures and two languages. At the end of his career, Millar wrote: "The underlying theme of many of my novels, as I read them now, is the migration of a mind from one place and culture to another. Its purpose, like the dominant purpose of my young life, was to repossess my American birthplace by imaginative means and heal the schizophrenic pain."[14]

When he finished high school, it seemed that Kenneth would never be able to attend college. He felt trapped in the basement of life: "I was measuring myself against standards I couldn't come up to. There was a strong sense of illegitimacy. I was in the wrong place, and it must be my fault. If the life around you can't contain your own thoughts, you carry guilt and a kind of explosiveness."[15] After graduation he worked for a year on a farm, receiving only his keep. He was rescued by the death of his father in 1932. John Millar died in a government hospital after a series of strokes, leaving his son a volume of Thoreau and an insurance policy worth some $2,500. At the time of his death, John Millar could not speak but was still writing verse. He had been unable to contribute to his son's support, and Kenneth had rarely seen him: "He condemned me to a life of emotional deprivation."[16] Nonetheless, the references to John Millar in his abandoned son's later autobiographical writings express forgiveness and a certain respect for the romantic failure's stubborn integrity.

Invested in an annuity, the small legacy was enough to put Kenneth through the University of Western Ontario in London, between Toronto and Detroit. He majored in English and history. From 1934 to 1939 he had nine appearances in the literary supplements of the *University of Western Ontario Gazette*—under his own name and as Keith Mill, George Beale, and Beames Anguish.

One day in 1935 Kenneth found his mother dead of a stroke. "We were very close, very good friends, much closer than I realized before she died. She had kept my spirit alive all those years."[17] Depressed by her death, Kenneth left college. He spent a year bicycling through England, France, and Germany while trying to write. In London he took part in an anti-fascist demonstration and was chased by a mounted policeman. Kenneth considered remaining in England, but felt that he would never be fully

continually. We of course got soaked even with the protection.

Our conversation was mostly about the grandeur displayed in our journey.

Our next route took us closer to the base of the mountains. Many streams or cataracts, large and small were leaping and tumbling down the mountainside.

Later, we reached the foot of the large glacier, but were unable to see it at the close view we had anticipated. The scene was magnificent. Huge snow peaks towered many feet into the sky. Others were surrounded by clouds. The glacier glistening in the sun, sparkled like a million diamonds. Great masses of ice rolled over the side of the mountains. Deep purple streams wound their way through icy crevices wedged in closely by snowy reefs. The glowing sun shone brightly on the glassy ice melting into little streams everywhere.

Very slowly, with great awe we made our way home with fondest memories of our trip through the Alps.

Impromptu

HE lay in a frail, crumpled, heap on the floor, beside his beloved piano, his long white fingers clasped behind him. Far away, he heard excited voices.

"What's happened? Who is he?"

"His song, wasn't it glorious?"

"He's dying, bring water! Don't stand there!"

Miguel smiled. It had been glorious, that impromptu! What would his maestro and his mother say? "Impromptu in C-sharp minor" by Miguel Consuelo. He could picture it, bound in handsome gold cloth—the initials would be red, of course. Then he would be famous, and his mother would gaze at him lovingly; and his maestro would strut up and down, with his hands behind his back and smile in approving surprise. Ah! that maestro—clod that he was! Miguel could almost hear his low, guttural tones.

"Keep on, my son. Practise, practise, practise all day long. And then, some day—who knows? You shall be a great pianist. But now—just a touch here, a touch there, yet." And Miguel had listened, and tried to understand. But "some day" seemed so far off; he was weary of practising till his long, white, fingers grew stiff with fatigue. What did they know of real music! He would show them—he would leave Seville—he would be famous! Dios! how the people would applaud and cry for more of his playing. Yes, to-morrow he would leave.

And so—Madrid, vast, cold, and unfriendly to young lads like Miguel, fired by ambition, and self-confidence. Where to go—perished by fatigue and hunger, and weak from over-exposure. He had played for everyone. And always the same reply to poor, tired Miguel—"Good, yes. But something vital seems to be missing. A touch of soul, perhaps." And Miguel strove for soul.

He had existed by begging pittances from passers-by, who had pitied the gaunt, young fellow. His cheeks grew hollow, and his long white fingers became stiff and chafed. Something missing, was there! Well, he would show them! He must, to live! He begged, he pleaded with theatre managers for just one more attempt. And lo, he succeeded! Rasping coughs shook his frail body as he entered the great playhouse. Trembling in every limb he sat down at the huge piano. Then suddenly music seemed to pour [from the] instrument, seemed to sw[ell and] burst forth in his very [own glor-] ious music! Surely, su[ch a] thing" was there, now. [He played] the song; his head felt [light.] And still he played, [to the] crowds. And then h[e saw] thousands of faces, sta[ring. He] thought of his mother [as he] showed them! Dios! h[e raised] his head, what a racking [cough] showed——them——t[he]

45

LEFT: The Grumbler, *1931*

BELOW: *Debating team, Kitchener-Waterloo Collegiate and Vocational School, 1931: Kenneth Millar standing fourth from right, Margaret Sturm sitting fifth from left*

"Why I sosceles produce a line."

"Oh, that is O. K. By the way, who is that Tan Gent Right Bi Sector?"

"G. O. Metric ptolemy that it was Con Current . . . ."

Suddenly the story was interrupted. Mr. Styles paused, then said to the class.

"Now take a piece of paper—sign it, and write out section Umpteen three times, letters changed each time, using a standard notation, Junior Geometry. May you have pleasant dreams. Good Night."

H. PATERSON.

The South Sea Soup Co.

THE ambitious young investigator, Herlock Sholmes, yawned behind his false moustache and poured for himself a cocaine—and—soda. He then lightly tapped with his knuckles a Burmese wacky-wara, which he had secured from an Oddfellows' Temple in French Indo-China. For it was thus he summoned his obtuse assistant, Sotwun. Sotwun crawled into the room, an idiotic expression on his face.

"I say, Sotwun, I'm sorry to disturb your reading of the 'Ju-Ju Journal' for March 1, 1927."

Sotwun stood awed by Herlock's amazing perspicuity and perspicacity. "How did you know that I was reading that, huh?"

Sholmes smiled and

's a min-esh plas-ournose. ce there r-of-paris in these rooms n the bust of Julius ext room, which I repaired Therefore your nose must e nose of the bust. As I ed your resemblance to a lly and mentally, Sotwun, must have imitated some w. The only picture in eople touching noses is in

the Ju-Ju Journal for March 1, 1927, which I scanned several years ago."

When Sotwun had overcome his astonishment, Sholmes explained the reason for his summons.

"Sotwun, has the South Sea Soup Company yet accepted my application for the position as head of their detective force, whose business is to discover oysters in their oyster soup? No? how strange!

Just then Herlock sneezed.

"Aha!" said he, "the 'phone!'

Instead of ringing, his telephone had been made to loose a quantity of gas when-ever there was a call. This gas had the peculiar property of causing one to sneeze. Thus Sholmes could be informed of the call without any undesirable noise.

He lifted the receiver. Immediately he recognized the voice of a man sixt-three years of age, wearing a brown suit and other clothes, who had been married eighteen times.

The strained voice said, "Mr. Sholmes? Oh! Come quickly to the office of the South Sea Soup Company. Mr. Ox-Tail-by has been murdered!"

Nonchalantly flicking an imaginary speck of dust from his eyebrow. Sholmes quickly undressed himself and donned his

RIGHT: First appearance in print: The Grumbler, 1931

assimilated into British life and was unwilling to abandon "that peculiar combination of qualities which we call Canadian but haven't yet fully described." After he became a novelist, Millar observed that "I suspect the intricate family plots in which my best years lie buried are peculiarly Canadian, and that they suture together the Matter of Britain and the Matter of America."[18] In Nazi Germany his pipe was knocked out of his mouth while he watched a parade, because he was smoking during the "Horst Wessel Song." His exposure to the Third Reich "confirmed me in being not so much left, but anti-right."[19] In some ways Millar remained "a man of the thirties," retaining an allegiance to the concerns of that decade.

When he returned to Ontario from Europe, Kenneth encountered Margaret Sturm reading Thucydides in Greek at the library. They were married in June 1938, the day after his college graduation, and honeymooned at the University of Michigan summer school, where he took three graduate courses in English. Margaret dropped out of college, and in 1938–39 Kenneth did graduate work in education at the University of Toronto to earn a teaching certificate.

In the spring of 1939 Margaret was pregnant. Kenneth had a job teaching English and history waiting for him at Kitchener Collegiate Institute, but the Millars had no money to get through the summer. Kenneth determined to write his way out. In need of a typewriter, he won one on a radio quiz program. He then wrote children's stories for Sunday school papers ("Marilyn Misses the Picnic" and "Abernathy the Squirrel") and bombarded B. K. Sandwell, editor of the Toronto *Saturday Night*, with poems, humor pieces, and stories. "Payment was just a cent a word, but the early joys of authorship were almost as sweet as sex."[20] In his first weeks as a professional writer, Millar earned over $100, enough to ransom Margaret and their daughter, Linda Jane, from the Women's College Hospital. He retained his connection with the *Saturday Night*; in 1939 and 1940 his byline appeared some forty times—in addition to many unsigned contributions in "The Passing Show" humor column.

The Millars returned to Ann Arbor for the summer session of 1940, and in 1941 he was awarded a fellowship on the basis of his straight-A record. (He had unsuccessfully applied for a Harvard fellowship.) The Michigan fellowship carried a stipend of $300 to $900 on the basis of need, but the Millars had a supplementary income. In September 1940 Margaret had been ordered to remain in bed for a heart ailment. After two weeks of reading mysteries, she decided to write one. *The Invisible Worm* was published by Doubleday in 1941, and she wrote four more novels in the next three years. Margaret's first books were humorous mysteries, but she later moved into the gothic/psychological genre.* Millar did not collaborate on his wife's fiction, but he served as her first reader and editor. He has acknowledged that he learned how to write a novel from editing Margaret's work and has credited her success with making his own writing ambitions seem possible.

W. H. Auden was a visiting professor at the University of Michigan in the fall of 1941; Millar enrolled in his English 135, Fate and the Individual in European Literature, an undergraduate course with thirty-two required books. Millar had admired Auden's verse and leftist politics for years, and English 135 expanded his grasp of literature, introducing him to Kafka and Kierkegaard. A notable mystery-fiction buff, Auden knew and liked Margaret's work. (When he came to visit, his voice upset two-year-old Linda, who had to be pacified with marshmallows.) Millar has perhaps over-generously identified Auden as "the most important single influence on my life."[21] Auden "set fire to me . . . simply by being exposed to a first rate writer who read my stuff and kindly advised me to cut the crap out of it was, I suppose, one of the four or five crucial events in my life."[22] Despite his own preference for the murder-in-the-village school, Auden "legitimized" the writing of detective fiction for Millar.

> Both Margaret and I were writing mysteries at this time. He was most encouraging to us. That kind of push is unbelievably important to a young writer. Auden was the greatest poet in the English speaking world at that time. It gave us a shove in the direction in which we were going anyway. It just couldn't have been equaled in any other way. It

---

* By 1979 Margaret Millar had published twenty-three books: *The Invisible Worm* (1941), *The Weak-Eyed Bat* (1942), *The Devil Loves Me* (1942), *The Wall of Eyes* (1943), *Fire Will Freeze* (1944), *The Iron Gates* (1945), *Experiment in Springtime* (1947), *It's All in the Family* (1948), *The Cannibal Heart* (1949), *Do Evil in Return* (1950), *Rose's Last Summer* (1952), *Vanish in an Instant* (1952), *Wives and Lovers* (1954), *Beast in View* (1955), *An Air That Kills* (1957), *The Listening Walls* (1959), *A Stranger In My Grave* (1960), *How Like an Angel* (1962), *The Fiend* (1964), *The Birds and Beasts Were There* (1968), *Beyond This Point Are Monsters* (1970), *Ask for Me Tomorrow*, (1976), *The Murder of Miranda* (1979).

W. H. Auden

marked a point in my life where I chose to become a fiction writer rather than a man who writes about other people's writings as a scholar; that's where I was headed. I would have done both, actually, but this straightened me out and put me on the creative path.[23]

Auden offered to introduce him to his New York literary friends, but Millar thought that it would be a mistake to go there under the auspices of a homosexual.

When Ann Arbor writer H. C. Branson published his first mystery novel, *I'll Eat You Last* (1941), Millar telephoned him to suggest a meeting. They became warm friends, and Millar remained an admirer of Branson's books about detective John Bent.

Millar did very well in graduate school, earning A's in all his courses and receiving his M.A. in 1942. He was a Rackham Predoctoral Fellow in 1942–43 ($1,000) and a teaching fellow and special assistant in English during 1941–43. After Pearl Harbor he tried for a commission in the U.S. Navy but failed the physical exam.

While completing his course requirements for his doctorate, he wrote his first novel in one month at Ann Arbor in 1943. *The Dark Tunnel* is a spy story set at a midwestern university and draws upon Millar's experiences in Germany. The author has described it as an attempt to treat a melodramatic plot in a realistic manner, with an unheroic hero. He has acknowledged the influence of Graham Greene on his early spy novels.

Margaret's agent, Harold Ober Associates, submitted *The Dark Tunnel* to Random House, which had become her publisher; but it was declined on the grounds that a husband and wife should not be writing for the same house. Published by Dodd, Mead in their Red Badge Mystery series in 1944, it went into a second cloth printing and was reprinted in paperback by Lion in 1950 and 1955 (retitled *I Die Slowly*). *The Dark Tunnel* received polite notice, but it does not foreshadow Millar's later work in the detective genre. The year 1944 was a good one for villainous Nazis, and the *New York Times Book Review* described Millar's novel as "a thrilling story told with consummate skill."[24]

By the standards of Millar's later novels, *The Dark Tunnel* is an unimpressive performance—with a Nazi transvestite and a locked-room murder. Awkwardly plotted, it utilizes crucial coincidence and a clumsy flashback. The writing is smooth and rather literary—after all, the narrator

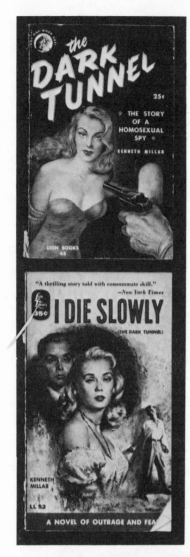

Paperback editions of Millar's first novel,
1950 and 1955

Jacket for Millar's first book, 1944

is an English professor. (Millar has remarked that sections of his first two novels were written in loose blank verse.) The ostentatious use of simile and metaphor that marks Millar's early novels is evident: "... a troop of SS guards like a mechanical black snake made of men. A brown caterpillar of storm troopers crawled behind them with breeches and leggings on its hundred legs. Then came a company of goose-stepping soldiers in army uniform, kicking out stiffly in unison as if they were all angry at the same thing and to the same degree. I had the grotesque vision of radio-controlled robots in field grey, marching across a battlefield towards smoking guns in pointed toes like ballet dancers and bleeding black oil when they fell down dead."[25] Although Millar would later attempt to diminish his debts to Chandler, their common heavy reliance on the simile is evident. "Every time Chandler would have a new book published, I'd dash down to the lending library—I couldn't afford to buy books at that time—and read right through it the first night.* I just can't overestimate the extent he influenced me at the time, turning me in the direction I took at that time as a writer."[26]

In 1944 Millar entered the U.S. Naval Reserve as an ensign. After officer's training at Princeton, he served as a communications officer on the escort carrier *Shipley Bay*, which was engaged in combat off Okinawa during May and June 1945. He felt cheated by his below-deck naval experience because he never saw what was happening. While he was at sea, Margaret worked as a screenwriter at Warner Bros., but her script for her novel *The Iron Gates* was never produced. The *Shipley Bay* put into San Diego and San Francisco; during shore leave Millar met Warner screenwriters Joe Pagano, Elliot Paul, John Collier, and William Faulkner —who impressed the Millars by his concern that his daughter's mare might foal in unsuitable California surroundings.

After the Japanese surrender, the *Shipley Bay* was used as a troop transport. While serving out his time, Millar resumed writing. He began reworking the start of a second spy novel, but broke off to write a short story at the urging of critic-novelist Anthony Boucher, whom he had met

* Chandler published four novels during the period of Millar's apprenticeship: *The Big Sleep* (1939), *Farewell, My Lovely* (1940), *The High Window* (1942), *The Lady in the Lake* (1943).

A BOLD STORY OF FIERCE DESIRE

NIGHT TRAIN

(TROUBLE FOLLOWS ME)

"ONE OF THE BEST BOOKS OF THE YEAR...
INTELLIGENT, TERRIFICALLY EXCITING."
—Albuquerque Tribune

Lion Library
35¢
LL 40

KENNETH
MILLAR

Cover of the retitled paperback edition of Millar's second novel, 1955

in San Francisco. It "wrote itself in two evenings,"[27] and won a $400 prize from *Ellery Queen's Mystery Magazine*. Millar credits this story with starting him as a private detective fiction writer. In "Find the Woman" (which Millar had titled "Death by Water") a Los Angeles private eye named Rogers is hired by the mother of a movie actress to locate her missing daughter. She is found in the sea at Santa Barbara, having been frightened to death by her returning Navy pilot husband who buzzed the raft on which she was engaged in adultery. Her mother, motivated by sexual jealousy, had intercepted the husband's wire announcing his return. "Find the Woman" remotely resembles Millar's Lew Archer novels in having a missing child as the triggering event; but it is a gimmick story of the kind familiar to readers of *EQMM*, although better written than most of the type. Millar has acknowledged "its obvious stylistic debt to Raymond Chandler. I suppose you could describe it as Chandler with onions. But then Chandler himself is Hammett with Freud potatoes. As Dostoevsky said about Gogol (I think), we all come out from under Hammett's black mask."[28] Millar published eight more mystery short stories, but the form never challenged him. His explorations of the backward and forward ramifications of crime—the web of causality—required more room.

During the same three-week voyage to Kwajalein that produced "Find the Woman," Millar completed his second spy novel, *Trouble Follows Me*. Published in 1946 by Dodd, Mead, it is built around a cross-country pursuit of Japanese agents, one of whom the naval officer–narrator falls in love with. *Trouble Follows Me* is another competent but unpromising work. Lion paperbacks reprinted the novel in 1950 and 1955, changing the title to *Night Train* and providing cover art that presented it as what was then called a "race novel" to capitalize on the episodes dealing with the wartime Detroit riots.

Margaret was on a train when she saw Santa Barbara for the first time. She got off at the next station and returned. When Millar was discharged from the Navy as a lieutenant junior grade on 15 March 1946, he was a Californian again. Instead of returning to graduate school, he wrote two novels before the end of the year "in a kind of angry rapture"[29] in an unheated stucco house on Bath Street.

One of the attractions of Santa Barbara was that it had a branch of the University of California; over the years Millar came to know faculty members Hugh Kenner, Donald Davie, and Marshall McLuhan—a boyhood friend whose course he audited at the Santa Barbara campus. Millar and fellow Canadian Kenner met in 1950, and the distinguished literary critic acknowledges his debt to the mystery writer's tutelage in narrative technique. Millar edited the drafts of Kenner's *Wyndham Lewis* (1954) and urged that he adapt the "sandwich" chapter method, which Millar often used: three scenes with the strongest one in the middle.

Santa Barbara was also a writer's town. Millar and Paul Ellerbe started an informal luncheon club that met biweekly for twenty years. It included Robert Easton, Willard Temple, Herbert Harker, William Campbell Gault, Dennis Lynds, John Merserau, and Irving Townsend. Easton, who became Millar's closest Santa Barbara friend, was a novelist who wrote on the American West. They shared a commitment to ecological concerns, and both served on the board of trustees of the Santa Barbara Museum of Natural History. Easton and Millar customarily previewed each other's work.

Blue City (1947) was declined by Dodd, Mead because it was too great a departure from Millar's previous work. It was accepted by Knopf, which published all his subsequent novels. Millar was proud to appear under the imprint of Knopf, the house that had published Hammett, Chandler, and Cain. He regarded Alfred Knopf as the best publisher in America. Millar also had the help of Ivan von Auw, his agent at Harold Ober Associates, who vetted the novels before submitting them to Knopf.

Blue City might well have been dedicated to Hammett; it is Millar's first hard-boiled novel and shows the influence of Hammett's *Red Harvest*. A tough discharged soldier returns to the Midwest of his boyhood to see his estranged father, the political boss of the city. But his father has been murdered and the crooks have taken over. Functioning as a lone redresser —much like Hammett's Continental Op—John Weather solves the murder (with the help of a good whore whom he rehabilitates), cleans up the city, and reclaims his father's kingdom. *Blue City* introduces the theme of exile and return, which Millar would develop with increasing complexity.

Millar's first attempt to write a hard-boiled novel, *Blue City* lacks a distinctive voice or point of view. The novel is told by the hero and thereby loses the perspective or detachment that Millar would later achieve by means of Lew Archer as narrator-observer. Millar properly insisted that the hard-boiled technique is more the result of style or language than of material or action.* "The mystery writer pretends, you know, to be writing hard-boiled, realistic material, almost something that has been written down verbatim out of somebody's mouth, and yet if you take a close look at it, you'll find that much of it is lyrical material; the characters talk a highly charged poetic prose. I think this is true of Hammett, and of Chandler, and of me too. You might call it romanticism of the proletariat."[30] In the hard-boiled novel there is brutality as the hero absorbs or delivers considerable punishment. ("Then I took each of his slender wrists in turn, and snapped it across my knee.")[31] But the distinctive element is provided by the stylistic response to the material: a matter of tone and point of view.

The hard-boiled style—more accurately, a combination of styles—was not the innovation of any writer. It was developed by many writers using the American language and the American experience in ways that fused in the late twenties and seemed to provide a voice for the bitter thirties. (Two of the masters of this American style—Chandler and Millar—were raised outside the United States; and Millar claims that his Canadian education sharpened his sense of American speech.) The evolution of the hard-boiled style owes much to Ernest Hemingway, but Hammett was publishing stories in *Black Mask* before Hemingway's work was known in America.† Millar has acknowledged that "Hammett and Crane taught me the modern American style based on the speaking voice."[32] When Millar was asked to provide a statement on Hammett in 1972, he wrote: "Hammett was the first American writer to use the detective story for the purposes of a major novelist, to present a vision, blazing if disenchanted, of our lives. As a stylist he ranked among the best of his time, directly behind Hemingway and Fitzgerald. As a novelist of realistic intrigue with deep understated poetic and symbolic overtones, he was unsurpassed in his own or any

---

* The earliest *Oxford English Dictionary* citation for *hard-boiled* with the meanings "hardened," "callous," "hard-headed," "shrewd," "of measures, practical" is an 1886 usage by Mark Twain; but the *OED* provides no example of the word as a critical term. A working definition of *hard-boiled literature* is: realistic fiction with some or all of the following characteristics—objective viewpoint, impersonal tone, violent action, colloquial speech, tough characters, and understated style; usually, but not limited to, detective or crime fiction.
† Under Joseph Shaw, who became the editor in 1926, *Black Mask* pulp magazine developed what would come to be identified as the Black Mask school of detective fiction.

OPPOSITE TOP: *Santa Barbara Courthouse*

OPPOSITE BOTTOM: *Harbor, Santa Barbara*

ABOVE: *Alfred A. Knopf with the Millars* (photo Hal Boucher)

time."[33] The hard-boiled technique is not limited to the detective genre, but it has received most of its development in crime fiction because the material lends itself to objective and understated treatment. Since the manner is easily imitated, serious writers of hard-boiled detective fiction have had to struggle for proper assessment against a host of hacks.

Blue City was published in the same season as Mickey Spillane's first novel, *I, the Jury,* which became a prodigious seller. Whereas Millar represented a continuation of the Hammett–Chandler tradition through respectful emulation, Spillane exaggerated the blatant qualities of the hard-boiled movement. Millar subsequently softened his work in reaction against Spillane.

The hardness of *Blue City* is at variance with the didacticism of the hero-narrator: "A city could be built for people to live in. Before I decided to leave or stay, I'd have to look for the good men who lived here. . . . Men with a hunger and a willingness to fight for something more than *filet* in their bellies, women in their beds, the champagne bubbles of power expanding their egos. Ten rounds by myself had beaten me down, but with good men in my corner I could last seventy-five."[34] Will Cuppy commented in the *New York Herald Tribune Weekly Book Review*: "The lad's social and political ideas stand little chance in this essentially teen-minded outburst, and they don't jibe with the rest of it any too well."[35] Millar would remain a moralist, but he would learn to sermonize by implication.

Blue City did not attract any special attention from reviewers. The *New Yorker* described it as "very, very tough, and a little silly, too."[36] The novel was condensed in *Esquire*, which pleased Millar because as a young man he had written to the magazine predicting that someday his work would appear there. Dell reprinted the novel in paperback, and it became Millar's first English publication when Cassell brought it out in cloth in 1949.

Millar's fourth novel, *The Three Roads* (1948), was another change of subject and style—or, rather, a continuation of his search for his authentic technique. It shares with *Blue City* the theme of exile, explored here in terms of an amnesiac's attempt to recover his memory. The novel bears an epigraph from Sophocles's *Oedipus Tyrannus*: "For now am I discovered vile, and of the vile. O ye three roads, and thou concealed dell, and oaken copse, and narrow outlet of three ways, which drank my own blood. . . ." The reference is to the place where Oedipus slew his father. *The Three*

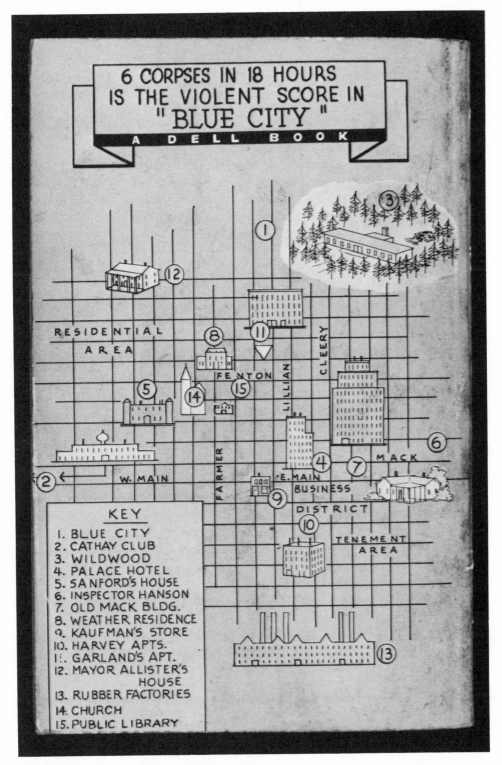

Back cover for Dell paperback edition of Blue City, *1949*

Roads thus announces the central myth of Millar's major work—but he was not yet ready to confront it. In fact, there is no oedipal quest in the novel. The hero does recover his "dead" mother; but she is not the object of his quest, and they never meet in the pages of the book.

In *The Three Roads* naval officer Bret Taylor searches Los Angeles for the murderer of his promiscuous wife. He discovers that he killed her, and has blocked the memory because of a childhood trauma. As a boy he believed that he had killed his mother after surprising her in the act of adultery. Millar's favorite doubling device is employed: Taylor thinks he killed his unfaithful mother, and some twenty years later he does murder his unfaithful wife.*

If *The Three Roads* was a false start on Millar's own literary and personal identity quest, it—together with *Blue City*—nonetheless marked the beginning of the writer's extended probing of concealed guilt as his characters attempt to confront or suppress the past. Past and present are intertwined, a point Millar announces through imagery and then explicates: "The shining metal streamliner waiting beside the station added the final touch to her allegory. It was the impossible future superimposed upon the ugly present in the presence of the regretted past."[37]

Millar failed to find an effective narrative framework for his material. His only third-person novel, *The Three Roads* has a limited omniscient point of view that is too limiting. Since the protagonist is searching for a murderer who is himself, the reader has a sense that the author is withholding information for the sake of suspense. The plot also necessitates flashback expositions by the woman who loves him—and who misleadingly conceals her knowledge of the murder. Though clumsy, the flashbacks are required by the third-person narrative. Knopf, who functioned as an editing publisher, asked for revisions in what he considered a slow-paced novel. Millar reorganized the first half to concentrate the action into four days and grudgingly cut "10,000 good words."

The plotting problem in *The Three Roads* can be partly blamed on the circumstance that it is two novels: a novel of psychiatric suspense and a detective novel. The *New York Times* reviewer was disappointed that Millar sometimes took "the Hitchcock fork rather than the Jungian

---

* *The Three Roads* was made into a Canadian movie, *Double Negative* (1980), which has not been released in the United States.

Brutal murder in sunny California is traced by a clue in the darkness of a man's lost memory.

Back cover for Dell paperback edition of The Three Roads, *1949*

curve."[38] To combine the requirements of both genres Millar employed a trick plot—that is, a plot that cheats or misleads the reader. In his apprentice novels Millar showed a fondness for plot twists. For example, in *The Dark Tunnel* the hero—as well as the reader—is led to mistake the woman he loves for her transvestite brother. As he gained experience and confidence, Millar refined the plot twist into the reversal. The twist is arbitrary, whereas the reversal is prepared for—even though it is surprising. The reversal or double reversal would become characteristic of Millar's plotting.

In *The Three Roads* Millar found his California locale, which would be the territory of all his subsequent work. The choice of setting was much more than a convenience, for Millar's California is conceived as the culmination of a social process. He later commented to Knopf, "Well, I always thought California would be a turning point in history—or a turning away point. . . ."[39]

After *The Three Roads*, Millar attempted to write a straight, or mainstream, novel based on his Canadian boyhood. "Winter Solstice" was about an adolescent being drawn into delinquency by economic pressure; but Millar was unable to control the emotions it aroused: "I tried, and got badly bogged down in sloppy feelings and groping prose."[40] Alluding to his Dickensian wound, he later remarked: "I left the manuscript, I think, in an abandoned blacking factory. The deadly game of social Snakes and Ladders which occupied much of my youth had to be dealt with in another form, more impersonal and objective."[41] The fictional mechanism that would allow him to handle the material would not be fully developed for another decade.

❧❧❧ TWO ❧❧❧

AT thirty-two, Millar wrote his first breakthrough novel, but didn't know it at the time. He was trying to write a novel that he hoped would sell: "I was in trouble, and Lew Archer got me out of it."[1]

Nevertheless, the first Lew Archer novel came close to derailing Millar's career, for the Knopf reader's report began, "I can't see much reason to go on publishing Millar." After characterizing the novel as a "boringly mediocre work," the report concluded:

> If Millar intends—and thinks he can—write a serious story, why doesn't he get to it? But if he insists on writing mystery stories, then he has got to come down off his high horse and realize that second best effort, at least *his*, just isn't good enough. My impression is that he thinks the mystery story really beneath him and that over-weaning conceit and pride keep him from realizing that even in this field a writer has got to work hard to get anywhere—at least one Kenneth

Millar has to. If we should lose Millar over this rejection—assuming that subsequent readers are no more enthusiastic than I am—I feel sure that our loss will be no greater than was Dodd Mead's when we took Millar over from them.[2]

On 2 September 1948 Alfred Knopf wrote reacting to "The Snatch": "Cut it any way you like, it is a big comedown for Kenneth Millar, not only from THE THREE ROADS but even from BLUE CITY. . . . But THE SNATCH —a perfectly impossible title of course, as I am sure you will understand— goes right back to ordinary, average, fair-to-middling run-of-the-mill stuff. Perfectly competently done to be sure and written in a superior style, but nothing that its publisher could hope to do anything out of the way with." In particular, Knopf found the ending in which Graves murders his million- aire father-in-law "unconvincing and thoroughly bad." He advised Millar to shelve the book, but assured him that the house of Knopf wanted to con- tinue as his publisher.[3]

Millar received Knopf's letter when he was packing for the move to the University of Michigan to complete his doctorate. He wrote to von Auw on the fourth, admitting that the novel was written as "a fast, color- ful, saleable book," but defended the plot under California's community property law. After Graves murdered Sampson he would be entitled to one- quarter of the estate.[4] Millar wanted to remain with Knopf, but he couldn't afford to scrap the novel. He proposed that von Auw shop "The Snatch" to other publishers under a pseudonym. After driving to Ann Arbor, Millar decided to offer the novel as *The Moving Target* by John Macdonald, telling his agent, "I doubt that I'll be doing any more straight mysteries." Although Millar insisted that *The Moving Target* was better than the average mystery, he admitted that "I am relieved that it is not going to be published under my name. . . ."[5] On the seventeenth of Sep- tember, Knopf agreed to publish the John Macdonald novel, provided that Millar would revise it to make Graves's motivation clearer. The advance was $500.

"John Macdonald" memorialized Millar's father, John Macdonald Millar. The by-line change was also partly dictated by Millar's wish to avoid the appearance of cashing in on Margaret's reputation. By 1949 she had published nine books and was much better known than her husband.

In October Millar reported to Blanche Knopf that he was revising *The*

Millar at the University of Michigan, 1949

Moving Target, writing his dissertation on Coleridge, teaching a composition course, and working on "Winter Solstice" during weekends. His main project was the dissertation: "When I've finished that I expect to teach half time, most likely in California, and write the other half of the time. I don't want to go on with bread-and-butter mysteries, you see, so I'm protecting my flank."[6] In a follow-up letter he told Mrs. Knopf that he hoped to write twenty books in twenty years. (In fact, he published eighteen books between 1949 and 1969.) Millar still regarded himself as a reluctant mystery writer, working under economic pressure while planning to break away into straight, or mainstream, fiction. At this time he began reserving the word *novel* for the nondetective books he intended to write.

In *The Moving Target*, Lew Archer is a Los Angeles private detective who operates a one-man agency. He is thirty-five years old and separated from his wife, who dislikes his work. Formerly a member of the Long Beach Police Force, he had been fired for his opposition to municipal corruption. Archer is intelligent, courageous, and good with his fists. He absorbs beatings and administers them; Archer vows to get one of his assailants and drowns him. If Millar had a model for Archer, it was Chandler's Philip Marlowe rather than Hammett's Sam Spade (who appears in one novel, *The Maltese Falcon*). Like Marlowe, Archer is a knight-errant, a free lance with a highly developed system of morality; but he is less romantic than Marlowe and, at the same time, more introspective in this first appearance.

> I used to think the world was divided into good people and bad people, that you could pin responsibility for evil on certain definite people and punish the guilty. I'm still going through the motions. . . . When I went into police work in 1935, I believed that evil was a quality some were born with, like a harelip. A cop's job was to find those people and put them away. But evil isn't so simple. Everybody has it in him, and whether it comes out in his actions depends on a number of things. Environment, opportunity, economic pressure, a piece of bad luck, a wrong friend. The trouble is a cop has to go on judging people by rule of thumb, and acting on that judgment.[7]

Marlowe doesn't find it necessary to explain his code of conduct. He does what he does for himself. But if the early Archer is righteous, he isn't self-righteous.

An unusually well-read man, Millar has acknowledged the influence of the Icelandic saga of Grettir the Strong, a tenth-century outlaw-hero, on his detective: "The hard-boiled detective story is, literally, epic in intention. These are sagas in which the idealized figure of the hero—Spade, Marlowe, Archer if you will—proceeds along a chain of events, a sequence of narratives, that ranges through a whole society and, hopefully, expresses it."[8] The name Archer is also borne by Spade's partner, Miles Archer, but Millar has said that the tribute was unconscious. (Millar was a Sagittarius.) Lew came from Lew Wallace, the author of *Ben-Hur*, because Millar liked the sound of it. The aspirational connotations of the name Archer are appropriate for Millar's detective, who is introduced in a novel titled *The Moving Target*.

Lew Archer provides what Millar has described as a welder's mask or a protective shield between author and material that is too hot to handle. Archer not only tells the story; his investigations cause things to happen and extend the web of causality. But he is not the hero; the novels are not about Archer. "He is less a doer than a questioner, a consciousness in which the meanings of other lives emerge. This gradually developed conception of the detective hero as the mind of the novel is not wholly new, but it is probably my main contribution to this special branch of fiction."[9] Millar had been impressed by "the talking voice" in Cain's *The Postman Always Rings Twice* (1934): "You can say almost anything about almost anything with a tone like that, I realized."[10]

Millar has remarked that "I wasn't Archer, exactly, but Archer was me."[11] His treatment of Archer's point of view allows both identification and separation: "I can think of few more complex critical enterprises than disentangling the mind and life of a first-person detective story writer from the mask of his detective narrator."[12] Archer is the voice of the author, but he is also the distancing character Millar has created. Millar might well have said that he wasn't Macdonald, exactly, but Macdonald was Millar. The pseudonym provided another layer of insulation between writer and material. If Macdonald is a persona for Millar, then there is a double-play combination: Millar to Macdonald to Archer. This idea is intriguing, but it is necessary to remember that *The Moving Target* was originally intended for publication under Kenneth Millar's name. Nonetheless, the Macdonald mask became an increasingly comfortable fit: "Archer, over the years, has become more myself, as I have become more myself. It took a good many

years for me to get into my own background and see it and reflect it."[13]
When the writer dropped Archer in two later novels, he retained the Macdonald by-line—though mainly as a marketing consideration.

In *The Moving Target* Archer is hired to find a missing oilman. (Oil-
men reappear as figures of corruption in the Archer novels.) The intricately
plotted case takes Archer through the Southern California underworld
of new money, easy money, dirty money. Santa Teresa, one hundred miles
north of Los Angeles, is the principal locale and is loosely based on Santa
Barbara. Although sense of place is strong in Millar's fiction, he does not
work close to his sources; he avoids the Gibbsville–Altamont approach to
fiction. Santa Teresa has the social ambience and moral climate of Santa
Barbara, but it is not a factual reconstruction of the city.

Millar told von Auw that "the basic evil" of Santa Barbara "is the
book's real subject."[14] He probably meant that it was about what money
does to people. Archer's cases come down to sex and money, and Millar
observed that all crimes are ultimately sexual. F. Scott Fitzgerald told
Harold Ober: "I have never been able to forgive the rich for being
rich. . . ."[15] Neither could the grown-up charity boy.

Millar regularly reread *The Great Gatsby,* which he has described as
"the closest thing we have to a tragedy illustrating our secret history."[16]
There are no admirable wealthy people in Archer's world, and the ways
they have acquired their money are frequently corrupt and corrupting.
Money is a main subject of the Archer novels. Whereas Fitzgerald's re-
sponses to the rich resulted in a simultaneous attraction and resentment,
Millar's response was single. The differentiating factor was that Fitzgerald
had grown up with the privileged in their own enclaves, whereas Millar
had been an outcast pauper.

The Moving Target is what the book trade calls a "page-turner"; and
Millar has described it as "a story clearly aspiring to be a movie."*[17] The
resolution of the novel demonstrates his management of the extended
denouement. The kidnappers are known by chapter twenty-four, but seven
more chapters are required to complete the novel; the principal murder is
delayed until chapter thirty. Millar has said that his books have more story
than the reader expects, and he has described his plotting as "a moral and

---

* It was made into the successful movie *Harper* in 1966. The title change was supposedly
dictated by Paul Newman's lucky-H superstition.

JOHN MACDONALD

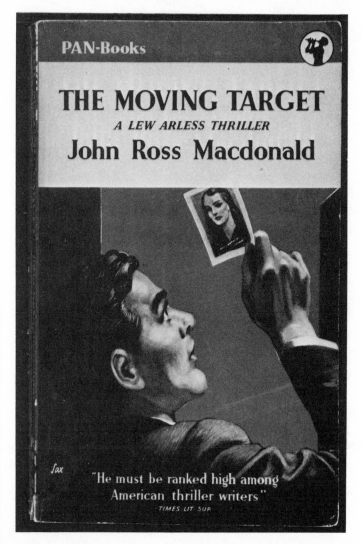

Jacket for The Moving Target,
*the first Archer novel, 1949,
and the first written under
the name Macdonald*

*First English paperback publication
of a Macdonald novel, 1954*

imaginative tontine."[18] That is, "I always start with an idea, and the idea usually contains in it the possibility of a strong reversal. . . . The reversal is actually an illumination of what has gone before."[19]

The writing in *The Moving Target* is a refinement of the hard-boiled style of *Blue City* to a style appropriate to Archer's sensibilities. Millar has explained: "The decision on narrative point-of-view is a key one for any novelist. It determines the shape and tone, and even the class of detail that can be used."[20] His reliance on imagery is still evident; but his similes become functionally symbolic—as on the first page of the novel: "The light-blue haze in the lower canyon was like a thin smoke from slowly burning money. Even the sea looked precious through it, a solid wedge held in the canyon's mouth, bright blue and polished like a stone." The people who live here not only have money to burn; their burning money has altered the atmosphere and transformed the ocean to stone. "I'm not just interested in a simile for the sake of what it does in the sentence. I'm interested in what it does in terms of the whole book. Some of my similes, I think, carry the message of my book better than anything else I write."[21] Millar has defined style as structure in miniature. However, some critics have cited him for an overdependence on the simile, a rhetorical figure that calls attention to itself.*

The Moving Target was well received, but it was by no means a best seller. There was only one Knopf printing, but the book was reprinted by the Mystery Guild in 1949—the first of Millar's ten selections.† Beginning with *The Moving Target*, Millar's novels were published in paperback by Pocket Books in America and by Pan Books in England—providing maximum rack exposure. In the cloth and paperback editions of *The Moving Target* published in England, Archer's name was changed to Arless, for reasons that are now obscure.

Knopf made a mystery of John Macdonald. The dust jacket did not identify him with Millar, and the author's photo was a silhouette. Millar's friend Anthony Boucher—who was not in on the secret of the pseudonym

---

* There have been major novelists—John O'Hara and James Gould Cozzens—who eschewed the simile, insisting that nothing is really like anything else.
† *Meet Me at the Morgue* (1953), *The Zebra-Striped Hearse* (1962), *The Chill* (1964), *The Far Side of the Dollar* (1965), *Black Money* (1966), *The Instant Enemy* (1968), *The Goodbye Look* (1969), *Sleeping Beauty* (1973), *The Blue Hammer* (1976).

but had correctly guessed John Macdonald's identity—welcomed the novel in the "Criminals at Large" department of the *New York Times Book Review*:

> Just at the time that the tough genre in fiction needs revitalizing, John Macdonald turns up. There is nothing startlingly new about Mr. Macdonald's plot (though there is great technical dexterity in his interweaving of three levels of criminal endeavor); kidnapping, contraband, decadence and brutality are familiar elements of the hard-boiled school. The outstanding freshness of this novel comes instead from the fact that Macdonald as a writer, as a weaver of words and an observer of people, stands head and shoulders above most of his competitors. He can evoke pity and terror for his "foreshortened figures with blood and money on their minds" and probe the social and psychological implications behind crime and detection—and do this without sacrificing for a minute the impact of a tautly paced, tightly constructed story. Macdonald and his Lew Archer (who pursues criminals while himself pursued down the labyrinthine ways) have given the tough 'tec a new lease on life.[22]

One reader who did not agree was Raymond Chandler. He wrote to the mystery reviewer James Sandoe soon after publication:

> Have read *The Moving Target* by John Macdonald and am a good deal impressed by it, in a peculiar way. In fact I could use it as a springboard for a sermon on How Not to be a Sophisticated Writer. What you say about pastiche is of course quite true, and the materials of the plot situations are borrowed here and there. E.g. the opening set up is lifted more or less from *The Big Sleep*, mother paralyzed instead of father, money from oil, atmosphere of corrupted wealth, and the lawyer-friend villain is lifted straight out of *The Thin Man*; but I personally am a bit Elizabethan about such things, do not think they greatly matter, since all writers must imitate to begin with, and if you attempt to cast yourself in some accepted mould, it is natural to go to the examples that have attained some notice or success.
> What strikes me about the book (and I guess I should not be writing

Raymond Chandler

Anthony Boucher

about it if I didn't feel that the author had something) is first an effect that is rather repellant. There is nothing to hitch to; here is a man who wants the public for the mystery story in its primitive violence and also wants it to be clear that he, individually, is a highly literate and sophisticated character. A car is "acned with rust" not spotted. Scribblings on toilet walls are "graffiti" (we know Italian yet, it says); one refers to "podex osculation" (medical Latin too, ain't we hell?). "The seconds piled up precariously like a tower of poker chips," etc. The simile that does not quite come off because it doesn't understand what the purpose of the simile is.

The scenes are well handled, there is a lot of experience of some kind behind this writing, and I should not be surprised to find the name was a pseudonym for a novelist of some performance in another field. The thing that interests me is whether this pretentiousness in the phrasing and choice of words makes for better writing. It does not. You could only justify it if the story itself were devised on the same level of sophistication, and you wouldn't sell a thousand copies, if it was. When you say, "spotted with rust," (or pitted, and I'd almost but not quite go for "pimpled") you convey at once a simple visual image. But when you say, "acned with rust" the attention of the reader is instantly jerked away from the thing described to the pose of the writer. This is of course a very simple example of the stylistic misuse of language, and I think that certain writers are under a compulsion to write in recherché phrases as a compensation for a lack of some kind of natural animal emotion. They feel nothing, they are literary eunuchs, and therefore they fall back on an oblique terminology to prove their distinction. It is the sort of mind that keeps avant garde magazines alive, and it is quite interesting to see an attempt to apply it to the purposes of this kind of story.[23]

Chandler's case is not strong. "Acned with rust" is a stronger image than "pitted with rust"; and "graffiti" is hardly an esoteric term. Nonetheless, Chandler correctly detected an inconsistency in Archer's language, which is occasionally more literary than his background would account for. Comparing himself with Chandler, Millar later explained, "My wider and more conscious vocabulary reflects a change in our living speech. . . . Chandler's hardboiled proletarianism has elements of self-stultification."[24] But

Millar's low-life characters do not speak the language of the streets. This was a time when "fuck" was still an obscenity rather than a commonplace; Millar's attempts to circumvent censorship are sometimes coy and inadvertently funny. In *The Drowning Pool*, published the next year, Archer reports: "He announced clearly that he would be fornicated with."[25]

"In order to have a democratic society, you have to have a classless language."[26] When this statement was queried by a friend who insisted that speech always stratifies the class of the speaker, Millar replied, "What I would wish is that the various strata should be available to the speakers of the language."[27] This issue identifies a problem in his technique. Whether the result of his Canadian exile or the result of his theories about the democracy of literature, Millar did not possess a sharp ear for American speech. Yet he was convinced that his printed prose retained the force of the spoken language.

Millar did not see Chandler's criticism until the letter was published in 1962. Although he judged that it was motivated by an aging champion's resentment of a young contender, Millar was hurt by it. Nonetheless, he continued to pay tribute to his early master: "He wrote like a slumming angel, and invested the sun-blinded streets of Los Angeles with a romantic presence. While trying to preserve the fantastic lights and shadows of the actual Los Angeles, I gradually siphoned off the aura of romance and made room for a completer social realism."[28]

Lew Archer would be the narrator in seventeen subsequent novels. It is not clear that he was created as a series character—or whether, having invented him, Millar found it convenient to retain Archer. There are obvious benefits and liabilities for a writer in maintaining a series character, and there is ample precedent in the mystery field from Poe through Doyle to Christie, Gardner, and Stout. (Archer—unlike many series detectives—is not an eccentric.) Readers like the reappearance of a familiar figure; and audience was a crucial consideration for Millar. He never aspired to be a mandarin author—despite his academic background. From the inception of his career he sought to write popular fiction: not for commercial reasons, but because his boyhood reading—reinforced by Frank Norris's "The Responsibilities of the Novelist"—persuaded him to seek a general readership.

The chief disadvantage of using a series character is that it takes pressure off the author. Instead of inventing new protagonists, he puts the same one through the same paces; and the reader's sense of familiarity may yield to boredom. This problem is largely obviated in the case of Lew Archer because he is the observing participant—not the hero. Millar does very little to fill in Archer's personal history in the subsequent novels. It is almost as though Archer has no life between cases. After *The Moving Target* Millar planned a "straight novel" to be called "The Defender," which he dropped. At this time he considered alternating Macdonald novels and Millar novels, but he stayed with Macdonald.

Millar received his doctorate in February 1952 for a dissertation entitled "The Inward Eye: A Revaluation of Coleridge's Psychological Criticism."* The 455-page dissertation "intends to mine Coleridge's critical work for a psychological theory of poetic, and to relate this theory to the psychological tradition in European and English thought."[29] It is an exercise in intellectual history rather than a critical study or a research project. Millar was gratified when he was told that his dissertation was the most distinguished ever submitted in the field of English literature at the University of Michigan. One observation seems to bear on his fiction: Great poems "draw the imagination through a process which finally constitutes this meaning. The process is the meaning. . . ."[30] The process through which Archer uncovers the layered past yields the meaning of the novels.

There were jobs for new Ph.D.'s in 1952, but the thirty-six-year-old Millar did not seek security in the groves of academe. He hoped to combine teaching with writing, if possible; but he was committed to fiction. Millar has remarked that he did not want to become like the members of his doctoral committee; but he retained a pedagogical impulse, teaching writing courses in the Adult Education Division of Santa Barbara City College during the fifties and helping to organize the Santa Barbara Writers Conferences. He developed a strong sense of responsibility about Santa Barbara writers. "We truly should be the Athens of the West," he told Easton.[31] (Millar was pleased when Constantinos Doxiadis said that Santa Barbara was the same size as ancient Athens.)

When Canadian Herbert Harker signed up for Millar's course in 1958, he had been writing for ten years with virtually no encouragement. Millar returned one of his stories with the written comment, "Your talent requires that you take up the work of a man of letters." They became friends out-

* See appendix.

side of class, and Millar advised him to read Pushkin, Turgenev, Dostoev-ski, Chekhov, Tolstoy, Gorky, and William Carlos Williams's *In the American Grain* to provide a base for his work; "Ibsen is a must."[32] In 1967 Harker began writing his first novel, set in Alberta, which he called "Early Winter." Millar read the working drafts and provided a new title, *Goldenrod*. Acknowledging his obligation, Harker later wrote, "He showed me what good writing was, but he never directly imposed his opinions on my efforts, so that what I finally ended up with was my own."[33] Millar's review in the *New York Times Book Review* observed, "Since a work of fiction is many other things, a record of the whole experience of creating it, *Goldenrod* can be read as a version of the author's struggle to become a modern man and an artist."[34] Millar was consistently generous toward other writers, as evidenced by the many blurbs he provided for their books.

Harker made notes on their conversations and preserved the following Millar obiter dicta:

> A story should be a circle.
>
> Causality. Everything is connected.
>
> Keep it a secret, like a gestation.
>
> Writing is essentially a private task, and for it to flourish, it must remain that way.
>
> The story is not the string, and it is not the knot. It is the undoing of the knot.
>
> When I find myself with an unsolvable problem, I sit and gloat for two days. It is in the working out of these problems, the building up to their solution, that the story comes into being.
>
> The control of ideas is only possible through language. And by practice we learn to use the subconscious so that it feeds into the conscious mind at the proper level. This is true of life as well as literature. Our symbols grow spontaneously, not by taking thought.
>
> We are all caught in the web of language. We cannot change it. All we can do is learn to understand and use it. It is a marvelous trap, of course. But we cannot escape it.
>
> The poet, when he uses a word, is conscious of its complete history— all the places where it has been used before—and uses it with all this in mind, then puts his own spin on it. The prose writer must also be

aware of the tradition of his language. The principal word in a paragraph explains that paragraph and provides its context, just as the paragraph provides the context for the word.

I think sometimes writers do better under pressure—stress. Not in the early stages of work. One can't stay in the air that long. But as we work to bring it all together, we need great effort, great concentration, as if we were preparing to pilot a suicide plane. . . . That's quite literally true. We want to consume everything that's *in us* at the time, in one great flash.

[On psychiatric problems] These can be overcome, won back, made productive. That is one of the great things we are engaged in—or should be engaged in—in our lives, the reclaiming of these swamps and deserts which are the result of our earlier experiences.[35]

Although the Millars never seriously considered leaving California, the attractions were the climate and the Pacific Ocean—not the life-style. The society appalled him, though it provided confirmation of his fiction. "Anything that fantasy can invent will find its real-life counterpart in California," he remarked after Bennett Cerf, Margaret's publisher, took them to a dinner party at Darryl F. Zanuck's house in Palm Springs. Millar had his picture taken with George Jessel by Moss Hart; Zanuck was shaved by a barber in his living room; and "John Macdonald was all eyes and ears."[36]

The Moving Target was followed by three Archer novels in three years—*The Drowning Pool, The Way Some People Die,* and *The Ivory Grin.* With *The Drowning Pool* Millar altered his pseudonym to John Ross Macdonald after John D. MacDonald protested.* Ross was selected because it is a common Scottish name.

The Drowning Pool (1950), dedicated to Anthony Boucher, introduces the themes of concealed parenthood and distressed children.† Since the daughter does not learn the truth of her paternity until the end of the novel, it avoids the child's quest for identity—which would become

---

* John D. MacDonald identified John Macdonald as Millar and wrote to Harold Ober pointing out that the by-line similarity was confusing readers and editors. Since John D. MacDonald was his real name, he requested that Millar choose another pseudonym.
† *The Drowning Pool* was made into a Harper movie in 1975, again starring Paul Newman, with the locale changed from California to Louisiana.

Lobby poster for The Drowning Pool, *1975*

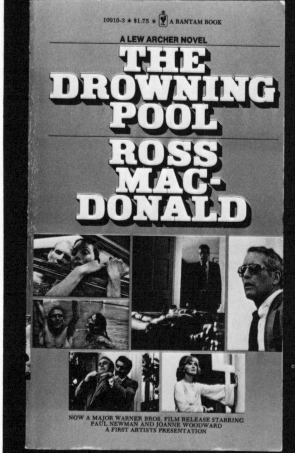

Movie tie-in edition, 1975

the dominant theme of Millar's fiction with *The Galton Case* in 1959. Millar asked Knopf to advertise *The Drowning Pool* as a murder mystery rather than as a novel of suspense—"a phrase which has acquired a rather vague connotation."[37]

In *The Way Some People Die* (1951) Archer encounters his first homicidal female as a missing-daughter case involves him in the drug racket. This novel marks the emergence of what some critics have discerned as Millar's misogyny. Most of his killers are women; they kill not for love, but for security. He has explained that women are frequently victims of society, and victims tend to victimize. The locale is Pacific Point, south of Los Angeles; Pacific Point resembles Santa Barbara in terms of social stratification, but is "a little more touched by the Orange County feeling."[38] Millar tried to alternate Santa Teresa and Pacific Point settings to avoid getting stale.

Boucher responded to *The Way Some People Die* with lavish praise:

> Macdonald has the makings of a novelist of serious calibre—in his vivid realization of locale; in his striking prose style, reminiscent of Chandler and yet suggesting the poetic evocation of Kenneth Fearing; in his moving three-dimensional characterizations; and above all in his strangely just attitude toward human beings, which seems incredibly to fuse the biting contempt of a Swift with the embracing love of a Saroyan. . . . the best novel in the tough tradition I've read since "Farewell, My Lovely" and possibly since "The Maltese Falcon."[39]

Chandler's novel was published ten years after Hammett's; Boucher was obliquely suggesting that Millar had surpassed Chandler. Millar was gratified by his friend's reaction:

> Since I write for you more than any one single person (even Maggie who tough though she is is tough in a feminine way and just a leetle repelled by the masculine sort) I'm naturally grateful for your good opinion of *Way*. I sort of have a sneaking liking for it myself, feeling as I do that I broke loose out of my personal neuroses in it and embarked on pure narrative for the first time. An element of smugness enters in from the fact that I've finished its successor (*The Split*

Woman) [*The Ivory Grin*] and you ain't seen nothing yet. No kidding.[40]

The Drowning Pool and *The Way Some People Die* reveal a sentimental streak in Archer that would be suppressed for a time. In *The Drowning Pool* he gives $10,000 to a hooker, along with the lie that it was left to her by a criminal who loved her. And in *The Way Some People Die* Archer allows the murderess to keep $30,000, for which she killed three men, to use for her legal fees.

The cast of characters in *The Ivory Grin* (1952) includes a syphilitic gangster, a corrupt beauty, and a deranged, puritanical doctor. Millar, who regarded it as his best novel so far, explained to an editor at Knopf:

> In my opinion, the distinctive qualities of *The Ivory Grin*, and the valuable elements in the convention from which it derives, are vividness and honesty of characterization, the close technical interaction of "narrative" or "drama," and plot; the amount of life packed into it; the chance at tragic passion. The physical violence which has become the hallmark of the "hardboiled school" has tended to kill it off with literate readers, and *Grin* was written in rather explicit reaction to this excess, the idea being to increase the psychological, social, moral range of the form while retaining the virtues noted above.[41]

James Sandoe came through with a warmly receptive review in the *New York Herald Tribune*: "Macdonald's sense of vivid similitude still overpowers him occasionally and he might now set to work to make his conversation as well heard as his milieu is well observed. But he is even now an admirably corrosive teller of tales and one of the few responsible and gifted practitioners in the hardboiled vein. It is possible to accept his creatures, tormented and twisted as they may be, as credible and worth compassion."[42] The Pocket Books reprint changed the title, without Millar's knowledge, to *Marked for Murder* because somebody there didn't regard *The Ivory Grin* as a "selling title."

The early Archer novels were reviewed with increasing appreciation as detective stories. Knopf sales were steady but not strong; of the first four

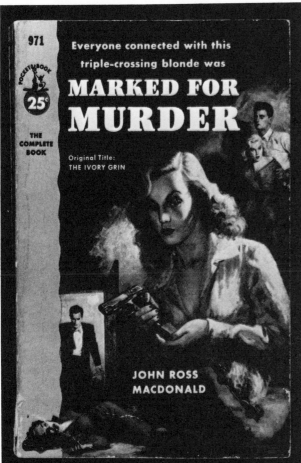

Retitled paperback edition of
The Ivory Grin, *1953*

Julian Symons

Archers, *The Way Some People Die* and *The Ivory Grin* went into second trade printings.* Although all of the Archer novels had been published in cloth and paper in England, his reputation was slow to develop there. Publication of *The Ivory Grin* by Cassell in 1953 elicited the first influential English review, anonymously written by Julian Symons for the *Times Literary Supplement*. Symons, a respected mystery novelist and critic, announced: "Mr. John Ross Macdonald must be ranked high among American thriller writers. His evocations of scenes and people are as sharp as those of Mr. Raymond Chandler, and the speed of his writing is almost unmarred by either sentimentality or sadism. . . . Mr. Macdonald's unusual merit is the ability to make an implicit social comment on the world he describes. *The Ivory Grin* uses many of the thriller's standard ingredients, but is not at all a standard product."[43] This review provided blurbs for subsequent English editions.

That Millar was publishing a novel a year after his Navy discharge does not necessarily indicate that he was writing too fast. He was a steady writer, averaging 1,000 words a day. The novels were written with ballpoint pen in spiral notebooks and turned over to a typist. (He worked on a writing board with his back to the window.) The typescript was revised and retyped until Millar was satisfied.

His novels were carefully planned; and he spent almost as much time on his notes for novels as on writing them, tracing the "relationships between people and events" that provide the plot lines. "I generally write about three different plots and develop them side by side to see which one I am ready to do. But then when I write the novel I sometimes use all three of them."[44] It has frequently been claimed that mystery fiction is plotted backward—that the writer devises the ending first and then works toward it. This generalization—which applies to some straight fiction as well as mysteries—has many exceptions, and its application to Millar is doubtful. Although his books end with one or more reversals, it is by no means evident that his narratives are constructed for the sake of a surprise climax. His plots are not Procrustean; the reader has the sense that the plots find their meanings in the process of composition. There is a strong likelihood that Millar began writing his novels with several possible con-

* The size of the Knopf first printings is undetermined, but 5,000 copies seems likely. The Cassell editions in England sold about 3,750 copies, and the Pocket and Pan paperbacks probably sold another 40,000 each.

clusions in mind, discarding alternatives as he progressed. His mind was fertile with plots, and by 1953 he had accumulated some twenty plot notebooks.

Boucher had urged Millar to try his hand at science fiction or future fiction, for which he could employ his wide reading in psychology; and in May 1953 Millar reported that he had a plot idea:

> It hasn't jelled and may not for some time, but if and when it does it will probably be a semi-political thriller . . . set in a society dominated by the techniques of the psychologists, educationalists, and communicators. The problem, apart from summing up the élan for a new departure and finding the time, will be to devise a vision different from the ones projected by Orwell et al. Plot is only a secondary problem, if I can articulate what I have foggily in mind: a Platonic society whose members and classes are differentiated by conditioned reflexes so deeply ingrained by training etc. that thought control is irrelevant i.e. the super-Eisenhowerian society. Through such a society moves a free agent who assumes the characteristics of each class in the hierarchy in turn, as he progresses towards the center of power where the completion of his mission (revenge cum political assassination) lies.[45]

He returned to this idea, but his pen went dead when he tried to write. It simply wasn't his material.

After *The Ivory Grin* he planned to alternate Millar books with Macdonald books, one each year. The Macdonalds would stick with Lew Archer; the Millars were intended to allow the author to depart from the private eye formula. His next novel, *Meet Me at the Morgue* (1953), was a non-Archer, but it was published under the John Ross Macdonald brand-name. (Knopf maintained the mystery of Macdonald's identity by accepting Millar's suggestion that an X ray of his skull be used for the author's photo on the dust jacket.)

Before Knopf accepted *Meet Me at the Morgue*, the publisher submitted it to Pocket Books. The paperback editor's reaction was lukewarm: " . . . for some reason all the books lack the kind of punch which should go with the sort of story he writes. . . . The sharp contrast between good and evil, so noticeable in Chandler's books and so important to this kind of story, is simply missing, at least for me. I wonder if some one of your experts couldn't somehow sharpen both the characters and the action."[46]

Millar responded to Alfred Knopf with a five-page defense of his work against the Chandler protocols.

Plot is important to me. I try to make my plots carry meaning, and this meaning such as it is determines and controls the meaning of the story. I know I have a tendency to subordinate individual scenes to the overall intention, to make the book the unit of effect. Perhaps this needs some correction, without going to the opposite extreme. This opposite extreme is represented by Chandler, one of my masters with whose theory and practice I am in growing disagreement. For him any old plot will do—most of his plots depend on the tired and essentially meaningless device of blackmail—and he has stated that a good plot is one that makes for good scenes. So far from taking him as the last word and model in my field, which Pocket Books thinks I should do, it would seem—I am interested in doing things in the mystery which Chandler didn't do, and probably couldn't.

His subject is the evilness of evil, his most characteristic achievement the short vivid scene of conflict between (conventional) evil and (what he takes to be) good. With all due respect for the power of these scenes and the remarkable intensity of the vision, I can't accept Chandler's vision of good and evil. It is conventional to the point of occasional old-maidishness, anti-human to the point of frequent sadism (Chandler hates all women and most men, reserving only lovable oldsters, boys and Marlowe for his affection), and the mind behind it, for all its enviable imaginative force, is uncultivated and second-rate. At least it strikes my mind that way. I owe a lot to Chandler (and more to Hammett), but it would be simple self-stultification for me to take him as the last word in the mystery. My literary range greatly exceeds his, and my approach to writing will not wear out so fast.

My subject is something like this: human error, and the ambivalence of motive. My interest is in the exploration of lives. If my stories lack a powerful contrast between good and evil, as Pocket Books points out, it isn't mere inadvertence. I don't see things that way, and haven't since *Blue City*. Even in *Blue City*, you may recall, the victim of the murder and the father of the "hero" was also the source of corruption in the city. Because my theme is exploration, I employ a more open and I think subtle set of values than is usual; its background is sociological and psychological rather than theological. I chose the hardboiled convention in the first place because it seemed to offer both a market, and a structure with which almost anything could be done, a technique both difficult and free, adapted to my subject matter, and a field in which I might hope to combine the "popular" and the "sensitive" hero, and forge a style combining flexibility, literacy and depth with the solidity and eloquence of the American-colorful-colloquial. These have been my literary aims; my hope is to write "popular" novels which will not be inferior to "serious" novels. I have barely started.

In spite of the Spillane phenomenon which has nothing much to do with the mystery but which probably has unsettled paperback publishers' notions of what a mystery is, I think the future of the mystery is in the hands of a few good writers like myself. The old-line hardboiled novel with its many guns and fornications and fisticuffs has been ruined by its practitioners, including the later Chandler. Spillane pulled the plug. I have no intention of plunging after it down the drain. My new book, though it is an offspring or variant of the hardboiled form, is a stage in my emergence from that form and a conscious step towards the popular novel I envisage. That very tone to which Pocket Books objects, and which I have tried to make literate without being forbidding, humane without being smeary, and let us face it adult, is what distinguishes it from the run-of-the-gin-mill mystery. It isn't as if I were out on a limb by myself. The fellow mystery-writers, and they are the real experts, think that my last two books [*The Way Some People Die* and *The Ivory Grin*] are the best that have ever been done in the tradition that Hammett started. While I don't think myself that I possess Hammett's genius—and that's a hard thing for me to admit—I do think that the talent I have is flexible and durable. My rather disproportionate (for a fiction writer) training in literary history and criticism which tended to make me a slow and diffident starter also operates to keep me going and I think improving. I do know I can write a sample of the ordinary hardboiled mystery with my eyes closed. But preferring as I do to keep my eyes open, I've spent several years developing it into a form of my own, which nobody can imitate. When the tough school dies its inevitable death I expect to be going strong, twenty or thirty books from now. As I see it, my hope of real success as a writer, both artistic and commercial, resides in developing my own point of view and narrative approach to the limit. . . .

. . . I don't quite see the point of the Chandler comparison, since this is not an imitation of Chandler. I like it better than a Chandler book, and think I can point out various ways in which it is superior to a Chandler book. If the characters are less striking, they are more lifelike, and the reader gets to know them better. There is none, or very little, of Chandler's glamor-stricken phoniness. None of my scenes, so far as I'm competent to judge, have been written before, and some of these have depth and moral excitement. None of my characters are familiar. They are freshly conceived from a point of view which rejects the black and white classification. The writing itself is fresh, and the imagery more integrated to the narrative with every book I write. The plot makes sense, and could actually have happened. . . .

I'm interested in creating moral excitement, which I think will be the successor to physical excitement.[47]

Pocket wanted to change the title to "The Convenient Corpse," which Millar regarded as a poor choice; he suggested "The Guilty Ones" as a substitute title. In the end *Meet Me at the Morgue* was retained.

Millar was depressed by his publishing situation. After six Knopf hardcover books he felt that he was in effect still writing for Pocket Books. Knopf submitted the typescripts to the paperback house before committing itself to publish because the reprint income was a key factor in the decision. Moreover, Millar was writing on speculation; he received no contract or advance until the book was accepted by Knopf.

Howard Cross, the narrator of *Meet Me at the Morgue*, is a probation officer who becomes involved in a case when one of his clients is suspected of having kidnapped a child. There is no compelling reason in the plot for dropping Archer; perhaps Millar wanted to demonstrate that he wasn't dependent on a series private eye. The substitution of Cross permitted the introduction of a love interest for the narrator. At the end he marries the child's mother, who has been widowed during the novel. The presence of a love story may have been why *Cosmopolitan* acquired condensation rights to *Meet Me at the Morgue.** The magazine titled it "Experience with Evil"—which also was the title when the novel was published in England.

With *Meet Me at the Morgue*, Millar's plotting tentatively began to seek more depth. A disgraced father trying to establish contact with the grown son he had abducted in childhood is introduced as a parallel to the kidnapping case.

Millar returned to Archer in *Find a Victim* (1954), a novel in which the killer is a deranged woman trying to preserve her marriage. Millar's victims are often self-victims, a thesis enforced by the epigraph from Stephen Crane: "A man feared that he might find an assassin;/Another that he might find a victim./One was more wise than the other." Although his plots are catalyzed by sex, the sexual encounters occur off the page— usually in the past. Archer is himself remarkably chaste for a fifties private eye. He does not bed a woman until *The Galton Case* (1959), and his couplings are not graphic. In the entire Archer series he sleeps with four women.†

Again Knopf required revisions; Millar admitted that he had over-reacted against Spillane and would try "to excise patches of wordiness and draw everything tighter to the narrative line, to harden Archer and his relations with his antagonists, to reduce explanation where possible, to render some of the crucial scenes more sharply dramatic, and to bring some of the sex and violence which is perhaps somewhat suppressed, into the open." The jolt of having to revise *Find a Victim* would be good for him, he said. "It strengthens my desire to become the world's best mystery writer."[48]

With *Find a Victim*—dedicated to von Auw—the identity of John Ross Macdonald was revealed. The back of the Knopf dust jacket carried the silhouette and X-ray pictures along with a photo of Millar, announcing: "Readers who have been puzzling over the identity of JOHN ROSS MAC-DONALD need puzzle no more. He is no other than KENNETH MILLAR. . . ." Boucher celebrated the disclosure by declaring that "the plot is more

---

* *Cosmopolitan* condensed six later Millar novels: *The Barbarous Coast* ("The Dying Animal"), *The Wycherly Woman* ("Take My Daughter Home"), *The Zebra-Striped Hearse*, *The Far Side of the Dollar* ("The Far Side"), *Black Money* ("The Demon Lover"), *The Underground Man*.
† In *The Galton Case*, *The Goodbye Look* (1969), *Sleeping Beauty* (1973), and *The Blue Hammer* (1976).

powerful and personal than earlier Archer stories—a strange and haunting blend of professional crime and private complexities. This is, in fact, so much more satisfactory, whether as a thriller or as a novel, than most other private-eye books that it seems to belong to an entirely different genre of its own."[49] Millar wrote Boucher that this review "brought tears to my eyes. . . . Your opinion makes me feel, know, that I'm not off in the wilderness by myself."[50] Boucher's statement may be regarded as the first shot in the battle to win recognition for Millar as a serious novelist. *Find a Victim* brought Millar his first notice in *Time*, which nominated him as the successor to Hammett and Chandler.[51]

Bantam Books became Millar's paperback publisher with *Find a Victim*. In 1955 Bantam published *The Name Is Archer*, a paperback collection of seven short stories: "Find the Woman," "Gone Girl," "The Bearded Lady," "The Suicide," "Guilt-Edged Blonde," "The Sinister Habit," and "Wild Goose Chase." These stories had appeared in *Ellery Queen's Mystery Magazine, American Magazine*, and *Manhunt*; and Millar revised some of them into Archer stories. He did not enjoy writing short stories because the form was confining. Two stories—"Midnight Blue" and "The Sleeping Dog"—were added to the 1977 collection, *Lew Archer Private Investigator*.

With *The Barbarous Coast* (1956) Millar settled on the pseudonym Ross Macdonald. Arguably his best novel to date, it explored the ramifications of power and corruption at a California beach club. In this novel he touched on his Canadian roots for the first time by introducing a Toronto reporter seeking his wife, but Millar was not yet ready to reopen that wound. Like several of his female victims/victimizers, the runaway is from a family that has lost its money. (Her actor father's movies as "Inspector Fate of Limehouse" had influenced young Archer to become a detective.) Another woman, the neurotic daughter of a movie mogul, is reacting against the death of her father and her husband's infidelities. Lost security —especially when combined with the loss of a father—is a powerful trauma in Archer's world. What critics would label Archer's almost Christ-like goodness emerges in this novel: "The problem was to love people, to serve them without wanting anything from them. I was a long way from solving that one."[52] The plot of *The Barbarous Coast* involves assumed identity, which became a favorite Millar reversal device.

ABOVE: *Jacket for English edition of* Meet Me at the Morgue, *1954*

LEFT: *Cover of the first Macdonald story collection, 1955*

BELOW: *Jacket for* Find a Victim, *1954*

After delivering *The Barbarous Coast*, Millar received a proposal from editor Ray Bond that he write non-Archer mysteries for Dodd, Mead—his first publisher—under his own name. The idea appealed to him because he didn't want to do another Archer right away: "I have a notion that when I do embark on a novel [i.e., a non-mystery] I'm going to get in deep and have to swim for my life. . . . But now is not the time."[53] The Dodd, Mead scheme was subject to Knopf's approval. Millar was not seeking a way to break with Alfred Knopf—whom he admired—but he was unhappy with the paperback veto situation. The decision was forestalled by domestic tragedy.

In February 1956 seventeen-year-old Linda Millar was involved in a Santa Barbara vehicular homicide. She was granted an eight-year term of probation in August and ordered to undergo psychiatric treatment.[54] Writing to von Auw in May, Millar included a message for Knopf: "You can tell him if you like that in and through this situation I've taken a step towards becoming the writer he would like to see me be."[55]

The Millars moved to Menlo Park, in the San Francisco Bay area, for a year. "Seismic disturbances occurred in my life. My half-suppressed Canadian years, my whole childhood and youth, rose like a corpse from the bottom of the sea to confront me."[56] (Millar thought, as well as wrote, in similes.) He underwent psychotherapy during 1956–57: "I had reached the point when I could not see anything clearly ahead. I needed help, and I got it. What it did for me was to take me deeper into life."[57]

Millar had large medical and legal bills to pay off; despite his problems, in 1957 he completed another Archer book, *The Doomsters* (1958). The title is from Thomas Hardy's poem "To an Unborn Pauper Child":

> Breathe not, hid Heart: cease silently,
> And though thy birth-hour beckons thee,
>   Sleep the long sleep;
>   The Doomsters heap
> Travails and teens around us here,
> And Time-wraiths turn our songsingings to fear.

Millar announced completion of *The Doomsters* by describing it to von Auw as "the culminating book (though not the last) in the Archer series. . . . My book is intended to close off an era—rather a big word, but I'm feeling my oats a little—in the 'hardboiled' field, and probably will.— My longtime and ultimate project is to find a place to stand from which I can fling some tenderizing salt on the tail of, conceivably, a small new Canadian or North American Karamazov or Quixote." He was disgusted by the sales of *The Barbarous Coast*. If Knopf didn't believe in *The Doomsters*, Millar was not eager for them to publish it. "Maybe we can find a better label than hardboiled, better sponsors than Hammett and Chandler. They're my masters, sure, but in ways that count to me and a lot of good readers I'd like to sell my books to, I'm beginning to trace concentric rings around those fine old primitives." The letter closed with a postscript: "I have decided to relinquish my amateur status!"[58]

Millar has described *The Doomsters* as "a work of tolerance trying to reach beyond tragedy."[59] It probes the past crimes that cause present crimes in a moneyed family. Again, the killer is a victimized woman. Carl Hallman, an escapee from the state mental hospital, seeks Archer's help. Hallman carries a heavy load of guilt. He holds himself responsible for the death of his father, Senator Hallman, because he argued with the old man, who had a heart condition; he also blames himself for his mother's suicide. His wife, Mildred—one of Millar's women from a declassed family —had pressured him into marriage because he represented security and restitution. "Money. That was what set him off from everyone—the thing that made him so handsome to me, so—shining." She describes her response to their sexual intercourse in blatantly monetary imagery: "I'd be in two parts, a hot part and a cold part, and the cold part would rise up like a spirit. Then I'd imagine that I was in bed with a golden man. He was putting gold in my purse, and I'd invest it and make a profit and reinvest. Then I'd feel rich and real, and the spirit would stop watching me."[60] Mildred, the least likely suspect, killed Carl's mother after a forced abortion and then committed three more murders—including that of the Senator—to protect her stake in the Hallman fortune.

The Doomsters, Millar wrote, "marked a fairly clean break with the Chandler tradition, which it had taken me some years to digest, and freed me to make my own approach to the crimes and sorrows of life." Chandler wrote connected scenes; but Millar treated "plot as a vehicle of meaning." Marlowe's voice is stylized and "limited by his role as the hard-boiled hero."[61] Archer has a wider range of expression because he is less encumbered by the requirements of his character and because a certain distance developed between Millar and Archer. Millar observed in a 1976 interview: "It took him [Archer] a while to develop into anything substantial. The real change in him, I think, occurred in *The Doomsters*; he became a man who was not so much trying to find the criminal as understand him. He became more of a representative of man rather than just a detective who finds things out."[62] The clearest way in which *The Doomsters* departs from Millar's previous novels is that Archer is personally involved in the events and might have prevented three of the murders. Some three years before, Archer had failed to help a drug addict who had witnessed the triggering murder:

> . . . I'd had five or six Gibsons with lunch, and I was feeling sweaty and cynical. My latest attempt to effect a reconciliation with Sue had just failed. By way of compensation, I'd made a date to go to the beach with a younger blonde who had some fairly expensive connections. If she liked me well enough, she could get me a guest membership in a good beach club.
>
> . . . .
>
> There was more to it than that. I'd been a street boy in my time, gang-fighter, thief, poolroom lawyer. It was a fact I didn't like to remember. It didn't fit in with the slick polaroid picture I had of myself as the rising young man of mystery who frequented beach clubs in the company of starlets. Who groped for a fallen brightness in private white sand, private white beaches, expensive peroxide hair.
>
> When Tom stood in my office with the lost look on him, the years blew away like torn pieces of newspaper. I saw myself when I was a frightened junior-grade hood in Long Beach, kicking the world in the shins because it wouldn't dance for me. I brushed him off.
>
> It isn't possible to brush people off, let alone yourself. They wait for you in time, which is also a closed circuit.[63]

Yet it is out of character for Archer to provide autobiography because his own life is suppressed. Millar told an English interviewer: "He lives through other people. He's the shadow of the novelist."[64] Thereafter Archer resumed his role as outsider.

Archer's involvement in this case generates his own guilt, which is expressed by a repeated metaphor of electricity:

> An alternating current of guilt ran between her and all of us involved with her. . . . The current of guilt flowed in a closed circuit if you traced it far enough.[65]

> The circuit of guilty time was too much like a snake with its tail in its mouth, consuming itself. If you looked too long, there'd be nothing left of it, or you. We were all guilty. We had to learn to live with it."[66]

The circuitry of the novel is closed by a linking dream theme. In the first sentences Archer is awakened by Carl Hallman from a dream of a hairless ape. After Mildred's confession Archer meditates:

> "I don't hate you, Mildred. On the contrary."
> I was an ex-cop, and the words came hard. I had to say them, though, if I didn't want to be stuck for the rest of my life with the old black-and-white picture, the idea that there were just good people and bad people, and everything would be hunky-dory if the good people locked up the bad ones or wiped them out with small personalized nuclear weapons.
> It was a very comforting idea, and bracing to the ego. For years I'd been using it to justify my own activities, fighting fire with fire and violence with violence, running on fool's errands while people died: a slightly earthbound Tarzan in a slightly paranoid jungle. Landscape with figure of a hairless ape.
> Thinking of Alicia Hallman [Carl's mother] and her open-ended legacy of death, I was almost ready to believe in her doomsters. If they didn't exist in the actual world they rose from the depths of every man's inner sea, gentle as night dreams, with the back-breaking force of tidal waves. Perhaps they existed in the sense that men and women were their own doomsters, the secret authors of their own destruction. You had to be very careful what you dreamed.[67]

Here is the clear declaration of Millar's departure from Chandler. The voice of Archer and the voice of Marlowe would henceforth be distinct.

Millar with Dorothy Olding (photograph © 1983 by Jill Krementz)

The reception of *The Doomsters* disappointed Millar, and he informed Knopf that he was "giving serious thought to the idea of changing my pace somewhat. . . . I have no desire to expend my powers on a form which does not seem, for one reason and another, to have attained the status I'd hoped for it; in this country, at least."[68] He did not forsake detective fiction; but his next novel would make a new start. After *The Doomsters*, Millar reported to Dorothy Olding—to whom he became steadily closer—at Harold Ober Associates: "On the very deepest level, or close to it, the new book is a diary of psychic progress. Not that I'm finished. Nobody ever is."[69] But before he was ready to write it, he had some money-making projects. He sent Olding an outline for a serial about atomic espionage in Canada he wanted to write for the *Saturday Evening Post*. He thought the idea had movie or television potential. Olding told him that it was a risky thing and advised him to condense *The Doomsters* for *Cosmopolitan* instead. The rewritten version with a simplified plot and a substitute killer appeared in *Ellery Queen's Mystery Magazine* as "Bring the Killer to Justice" in 1962. At this time Millar found himself writing verse after a twenty-year layoff and expected to have enough for a book in a year or two. He described the material as "mostly rather philosophic and obscure, about Plato and Descartes and things."[70] These poems were not published.

In August 1957, Dodd, Mead revived the idea for a series of mysteries "by Kenneth Millar"; and Millar wanted to write the atomic spy story—subject to Alfred Knopf's approval. Since Millar was still paying off his debts, he required a contract from Dodd, Mead "for the first time in my life" and a decent advance.[71] Von Auw agreed to explore the matter with Knopf, but nothing came of it.

Between 1958 and 1960 Millar wrote some forty-five book reviews for the *San Francisco Chronicle*. He had no formal connection with the paper, and the reviews were written for pleasure. As a critic he was more than fair, never attacking for the fun of it. He did not review detective fiction, and most of his articles dealt with literary criticism or biography. Reviewing A. E. Murch's *The Development of the Detective Novel*, he rejected the traditional, or English, position that the mystery is at its best when it deals with scientific detection. He argued that the mystery novel is a novel —not just a mystery—and belongs in the literary mainstream where it can deal with the realities of life.[72] The only book that moved Millar to mild irritation was a biography of Stephen Leacock—one of his boyhood models —because it did not do justice to the writer who had "loved and ornamented the Anglo-American-Canadian language."[73]

~~~ THREE ~~~

MILLAR has stated that his year of psychiatric treatment "marked the difference between my early and later books. There's no question that my work has deepened since then. Freud was one of the two or three greatest influences on me. He made myth into psychiatry, and I've been trying to turn it back into myth again in my own small way."[1] Millar healed himself by writing *The Galton Case* (1959), his second breakthrough book—ten years after *The Moving Target*: "I learned what every novelist has to learn: to convert his own life as it grows into his fiction as he writes."[2] Psychotherapy freed him to confront his childhood in his thirteenth novel, written at forty-two during the winter of 1957–58. While writing what became *The Galton Case*, he told Alfred Knopf that it was "planned as a transition out of the 'hard-boiled' realm. . . . my ambition for these coming years is to write on serious themes, not necessarily lugubrious ones, with a simplicity and speed and perhaps bravura which all of my books have had in some degree. I aim at *narrative* beauties, which seem to be rather rare these days."[3]

Millar reconstructed the gestation and composition in "A Preface to *The Galton Case*" (1968):

> The central idea which was to magnetize the others and set them in order was a variation on the Oedipus story. It appears in the red notebook briefly and abruptly, without preparation: "Oedipus angry vs. parents for sending him away into a foreign country."*
>
> This simplification of the traditional Oedipus stories, Sophoclean or Freudian, provides Oedipus with a conscious reason for turning against his father and suggests that the latter's death was probably not unintended. It rereads the myth through the lens of my own experience, and this is characteristic of my plots.[4]

Before he wrote the novel there were at least three false starts, each narrated by a boy whose situation suggests aspects of Millar's Canadian boyhood. The early working titles were "A Matter of Identity," "The Castle and the Poorhouse," and "The Imposter"—all suggesting the theme of exclusion or displacement. The first start reported an encounter between the Canadian boy and an American who mentions the possibility of hiring him. It died on page 13 because of inadequate planning and because the boy wasn't able to tell his complicated story: "Neither structure nor style was complex enough to let me discover my largely undiscovered purposes."[5]

In the second start the boy is anticipating an appointment with a Mr. Sablacan at the Royal York Hotel in Toronto. It ends on page 6 with a family breakfast scene, revealing the point at which Millar embraced his myth. Or it seized him.

> . . . I sat and ate my breakfast in silence. With the old man propped up opposite me; eyes closed and mouth open, it was a little like eating with a dead man at the table.
>
> Something had broken in him long ago. He was a drunken bum. My father was a drunken bum. That was what I couldn't forgive him for.

* Used in chapter twenty-four.

The old lady forgave him, though. The lower he sank, the better she treated him. She cooked his meals and washed his clothes and worked an eight-hour day at the dairy to support him. She even gave him money for wine, and sometimes she let him beat her.

My aunts and uncles on her side of the family said that she was a saint, a foolish saint to put up with him all these years. I was beginning to wonder about that. I had a vague suspicion that maybe she had broken down, too. Maybe the two of them had broken down together, when she took the ball away from him and started running with it.

I think that morning was the closest I'd ever come to sympathizing with the old man. But I still had to get away from him. I had to get away from her, too.

She'd go on feeding me until I choked. She'd be pouring me cups of tea until I drowned in the stuff. She'd give me loving encouragement until I suffocated.

At the bottom of this page the author added a note: "[Aug. 1967—My story had begun to feed on its Oedipal roots.]"[16]

Despite its brevity, Millar felt that this beginning enabled him to structure his narrative.

Version Two was a good deal more than a false start. Swarming with spontaneous symbolism, it laid out one whole side, the sinister side, of the binocular vision of my book. In fact, it laid it out so completely that it left me, like Willie [the narrator], nowhere to go but away. I couldn't begin the novel with the infernal vision on which part of its weight would finally rest; the novel must converge on that gradually. But by writing my last scene first, in effect, and facing its Medusa images—poverty and family failure and hostility—my imagination freed itself to plan the novel without succumbing to the more obvious evasions.[7]

Millar's account does not mention a third start set in Toronto, twenty-eight pages in which the narrator is interrogated by Sablacan and taken to meet a couple who offer him the opportunity to make a great deal of money.

Your father is a disappointed man. He didn't have your advantages, I can tell you."

I was getting sick and tired of being reminded of my advantages. But I didn't say anything to her. I sat and ate my breakfast in silence. With the old man propped up opposite me, eyes closed and mouth open, it was a little like eating with a dead man at the table.

Same?

Something had broken in him long ago. He was a drunken bum. My father was a drunken bum. That was what I couldn't forgive him for. The old lady could forgive him, though. The lower he sank, the better she treated him. She cooked his meals and washed his clothes and worked an eight-hour day at the dairy to support him. She even gave him money for wine, and sometimes she let him beat her.

My aunts and uncles on her side of the family said that she was a saint, a foolish saint to put up with him all these years. I was beginning to wonder about that. I had a vague suspicion that maybe she had broken down, too. Maybe the two of them had broken down together, when she took the ball away from him and started running with it.

I think that morning was the closest I'd ever come to sympathizing with the old man. But I still had to get away from him. I had to get away from her, too.

She'd go on feeding me until I choked. She'd be pouring me cups of tea until I drowned in the stuff. She'd give me loving encouragement until I suffocated.

[Aug. 1967— My story had begun to feed on its Oedipal roots.]

Preliminary draft for The Galton Case
(Special Collections, University Library, University of California, Irvine)

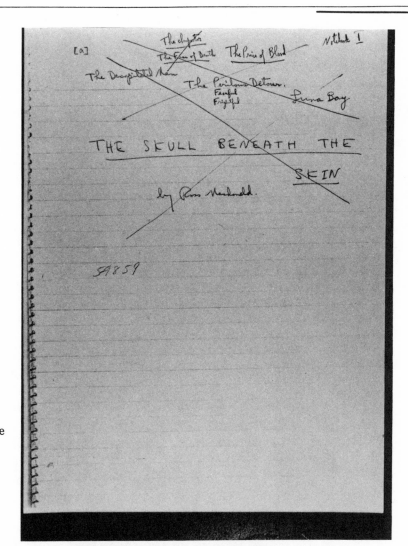

Trial titles for The Galton Case
(Special Collections,
University Library,
University of California,
Irvine)

*Jacket for Millar's break-
through novel, 1959*

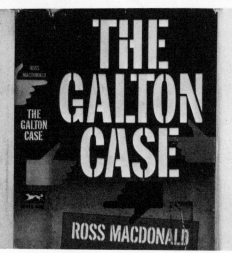

ROSS MACDONALD

THE
GALTON
CASE

ROSS
MACDONALD

THE
GALTON
CASE

While he was planning the novel, Millar lived near Donald Davie, who was adapting into English Mickiewicz's classic Polish poem *Pan Tadeusz*, about a son seeking an unknown father.*

> *The Galton Case* turns on the same typical situation, and my talks with Ken had to do with what a common, apparently archetypal plot this is (Walter Scott's *Waverly* was one case we considered), and on how Freudian and other psychology explained why the plot was so continually recurrent, and how meaningful it is, in our age as in the age of Walter Scott and Mickiewicz. Ken's talk about this showed clearly how he was concerned to use the "thriller" form to explore and confirm and reinterpret significances known to us from the epic literature of the past.[8]

Millar felt that Davie "sort of sparked the writing of *The Galton Case.*"[9]

The first draft was called "The Enormous Detour" (later, "The Grand Detour"). Other rejected titles for *The Galton Case* were "The Fear of Death," "The Price of Blood," "The Decapitated Man," "The Perilous Detour," "The Fearful Detour," "The Frightful Detour," "Luna Bay," and "The Skull Beneath the Skin" (from T. S. Eliot's "Whispers of Immortality"). In the first version Millar made the crucial decision to use Archer as the narrator: ". . . I made up my mind that the convention of the detective novel, in which I had been working for fifteen years, would be able to contain the materials of my most ambitious and personal work so far. I doubt that my book could have been written in any other form." When his friend John Merserau read "The Enormous Detour," he advised Millar that it "could not succeed as a novel unless it succeeded in its own terms as a detective novel." Millar then went back to the second false start and wrote a new ending from the breakfast scene—"leading me into the heart of my subject not just once but again."[10]

The Galton Case opens when Archer is called in by lawyer Gordon Sable (an echo of Sablacan) to trace the long-lost son of wealthy Mrs. Galton. In the first chapter there is a simile Millar was proud of because it demonstrates how style functions as "structure on a small scale."[11] When

---

* *The Forests of Lithuania* (London: Marvel Press, 1959).

Archer gets up from the Harvard chair in Sable's office, he remarks, "It was like being expelled."[12] On an obvious level this wisecrack identifies Archer with the have-nots; but it also introduces the theme of expulsion that reverberates through *The Galton Case* and its successors. "I've deepened the use of imagery. I've changed it from the imagist to the symbolist, where it is intended to have deep psychological and social meanings."[13]

The novel begins as a quest for Anthony Galton, who in 1936 had renounced his affluent family to become a proletarian writer under the name John Brown. He took a lower-class wife and disappeared. Millar attributed one of his own poems—written when he was nineteen—to Brown. The sixteen-line "Luna" opens:

> While her breast
> As the white foam
> Where the gulls rest
> Yet find no home....

Archer discovers the long-buried decapitated skeleton of Anthony Galton and at the same time finds a young man who claims to be Galton's son, John Brown, Jr. His story is unverifiable: he was abandoned in an orphanage that has burned down. Mrs. Galton accepts the claimant as her grandson and discharges Archer. But Archer is troubled. For one thing, it has been too easy—the pieces have fallen together too quickly. Moreover, an apparently unrelated murder occurs at Sable's home. His houseman, Culligan, is stabbed by an unknown assailant; and Archer is brutally beaten by Nevada gangsters when he follows up the Culligan murder. Archer does not like unexplained coincidences. He decides to stick with the case. Following the trail backward, he determines that young Brown/Galton is Theodore Fredericks, an impostor planted by Sable—in collusion with Culligan—to retain control of the Galton fortune. The trail takes Archer to Canada, where he locates the impostor's family and establishes that, even though he doesn't know it, Theodore Fredericks really is the Galton grandson. Anthony Galton had been murdered by his wife's former lover, an escaped convict named Shoulders Nelson (Nelson Fredericks). She had gone to Canada with Nelson, who would otherwise have killed the infant; and the boy had been raised to believe he was Nelson's son. Nelson has become a broken-down alcoholic, partly as a result of the stab wound delivered by his ostensible son. "Like the repeated exile of Oedipus, the crucial events of my novel seem to happen at least twice. And like young Oedipus, [Theodore] is a 'son' who appears to kill a 'father,' thus setting the whole story in circular motion."[14]

The pastness of the present provides the structural rationale for Millar's best plots. Millar proposed to Knopf that *The Galton Case* be billed as "A Novel of Identity" and "perhaps in the jacket copy to present the book as a payoff of a fifteen-year effort to write a popular novel with a powerful plot which also has the qualities of serious narrative; a novel which speaks directly to people about contemporary life without talking down—or talking up, either." His recognition that he had surpassed his previous work is further supported by Millar's suggestion that he provide "a short critical preface or letter stating the intention of my work and linking it up, as I am well qualified to do, with literary history and the problem found by American writers from Poe on down, and crucial now, of what audience and level of language to commit themselves to."[15] His offer was not accepted, but he provided flap copy that may have been used for the dust jacket:

> In the past dozen years, Ross Macdonald has emerged as one of our most original writers of adult mystery stories. A growing number of readers here and abroad know him as a novelist of explosive excitement. Among fellow-writers and critics he is coming to be recognized as a rising master of a complex and colorful art. The "hard-boiled" label that has often been applied to Macdonald's books does them a disservice: the fact is that they bear only a superficial resemblance to the standard hard-boiled product. Critics use such words as "creative, subtle, compassionate, literate, meaningful," to describe them. Yet these words of praise are earned without sacrificing drive and bite, staccato pace, and some of the wickedest plotting ever perpetrated.
>
> *The Galton Case* is perhaps Macdonald's most brilliantly plotted book to date, and certainly his most deeply felt one. For the first time Lew Archer discovers love and hope at the heart of the human tragedy. We feel that this book achieves a new maturity. It speaks to people of

all sorts, powerfully and imaginatively about the basic hopes and dreads of life.

The quest for identity—frequently in the form of paternity quest—is the moving force in most of Millar's subsequent novels. Although this theme had been foreshadowed as early as *Blue City* and *The Three Roads*, Millar was unable to confront it until *The Galton Case* freed him to deal with the ghosts on the battlements of his Canadian Elsinore.

The principal reviews of *The Galton Case* were relegated to the mystery-crime departments, and there was no recognition that the novel marked the inception of a new direction in Millar's fiction. Series detective novels rarely attract prominent critical attention, and reviewers tend to assess them in terms of one another. Thus: Macdonald meets his usual high standard. Or: Macdonald surpasses his usual high standard. When the writer breaks new ground it may not be noticed. Boucher quoted the dust jacket blurb and remarked that "Macdonald has been this good for ten years now, and I'm glad his publisher has finally noticed it."[16] The *Times Literary Supplement* identified one of Millar's main strengths: "Mr. Macdonald has fortunately reached the ultimate sophistication in this *genre*: he is able to spread his post-climax explanations over a good many pages and still reserve a punch for the last paragraph."[17] The sales were routine—two Knopf printings in 1959 and one Bantam paperback printing in 1960.

The Galton Case is a novel about a pauper prince, in which the differences between having and not having are emphasized by the sociology of California. Millar's residence in an old-money city with a marked social stratification re-enforced his awareness of barriers. There is a considerable burden of social commentary in his work. Although Archer is usually employed by the affluent, his sympathies are with the deprived. Writer and narrator manifest a bias against privilege. Millar commented that Archer is less radical than he; but there are implicit political messages in the Archer books. The writer's opposition to the corruption of power is manifest in his treatment of tycoons and racketeers—between whom there is usually little to choose. His own political illusions did not survive the disappointment of the 1952 Stevenson–Eisenhower election. He was so confident of Stevenson's victory that at first he thought the election returns were a hoax.

Thereafter the Millars were active in environmental causes. He participated in the effort to preserve the nesting area of the California condor and wrote two articles for the cause.* Both he and Margaret were ardent birdwatchers, and she wrote a nonfiction account of their initiation into bird lore in *The Birds and Beasts Were There* (1968). It was intended as a collaboration, but he dropped out. They were also trial watchers, spending a good deal of time in court observing murder cases: "The antagonist system, combined with the professional blood thirstiness of prosecutors, works to the disadvantage of the already disadvantaged. They are punished for being poor and stupid and sick."[18]

Margaret was a morning writer, and Kenneth wrote in the afternoon; they worked in different parts of the house. Their only collaboration was on an unproduced television script. A husband and wife writing novels in the same field provides a stereotypical situation for ego rivalry, and S. J. Perelman wrote a burlesque based on the Millars.† But Kenneth and Margaret were never in competition with each other, partly because their work was so different. In the early years he was proud of her greater success, and she did not resent it when he became the literary star of the family in the seventies—by which time her output had slacked off. "I honestly believe that Margaret's the best in the business," he reiterated.[19]

In the early sixties the Millars' joint income was between $12,000 and $15,000 a year. Their living habits were perforce simple, even frugal. They did their own housework; Millar ate plain food, which he often prepared for himself; and his clothes came from J. C. Penney's. He usually wore a plaid shirt and a baseball cap. When they ate out, it was customarily at the Copper Coffee Pot, a cafeteria on State Street. The Millars devoted their nonwriting time to reading, walking, bicycling, and year-round swimming. In his younger years Millar enjoyed platform diving. Threatened with a wheelchair by recurrent gout, he took long walks as therapy. They were devoted to their dogs, one of whom refused to be left alone in the house. When the Millars went out together, Brandy remained in the parked car, and Millar would go out to reassure him. Millar quit smoking because he

---

* "A Death Road for the Condor," *Sports Illustrated*, 6 April 1964, pp. 86–89; "The Slow Death of the California Condor," *San Francisco Chronicle—This World*, 12 May 1968, p. 34.
† "Oh, I Am a Cook and a Houseboy Bland," *The New Yorker*, 8 February 1961, pp. 34–37.

Birdwatching, 1972 (photo
Rafael Maldonado, Jr.,
Santa Barbara News-Press)

*Kenneth Millar in Santa Barbara
Courthouse* (photograph © 1983
by Jill Krementz)

wanted to live as long as possible, and he became a chain-chewer of fruit-flavored sugarless gum. After Margaret was operated on for lung cancer, they became militant antismokers.

The movie money for *The Moving Target* allowed the Millars to buy a house (with a naked mermaid painted on the bottom of the swimming pool) in the affluent Hope Ranch section of Santa Barbara in 1965, which provided access to a private beach. Millar rationalized the $90,000 purchase—which was a good deal of money then—by explaining that it would compel him to keep writing. Among the pleasures of their property on Via Esperanza were the bird and animal life. They were also members of the Coral Casino Beach Club, which has an olympic-size saltwater pool.

On 30 May 1959, nineteen-year-old Linda Millar signed out of her dormitory at the University of California, Davis, and went to a casino in Stateline, Nevada. Shortly after midnight she told her companions that she had to get back before curfew and would hitchhike. She never got back to school. Her father reported that she had been recently troubled by guilt feelings about her 1956 vehicular homicide experience. He hired private detectives and actively participated in the search, making television appeals for Linda to contact her parents. When a check cashed by her in a Los Angeles supermarket was reported, Millar delivered a message through the press: "I cried with joy and relief when I learned that you are alive. . . . You're the person we love most. Did you ever doubt it? You're afraid; you must be afraid or you'd have come home long since. Believe me there's nothing to be afraid of. . . . Faith can move mountains, you know, but most of the mountains you may feel you have to climb alone are mole hills under a magnifying glass and you're not going to have to climb them alone. . . . I am 100 per cent for you and I wouldn't trade you for any other daughter in the world. . . ." She was found in Reno on the tenth of June, but had only a dim memory of where she had been.[20] The figure of Linda Millar can be perceived behind the troubled girls in her father's novels. Richard Schickel has observed that Millar was the first writer to employ the generation gap as a subject for detective fiction. After Linda's return Millar was hospitalized for hypertension, and Robert Easton was concerned that he might never recover. Millar fought back with the help of nine different daily medications.

Having unearthed the roots of his fiction in his boyhood exile and having proved that the painful material could be handled through Archer's

*Margaret Millar with
Brandy, 1964* (photo
Hal Boucher)

Millar in 1972 (photo
Santa Barbara News-Press)

On the beach at Santa Barbara
(photograph © 1983
by Jill Krementz)

*Kenneth and Margaret with
Brandy* (photograph © 1983
by Jill Krementz)

In the Pacific (photograph © 1983 by Jill Krementz)

Kenneth and Margaret with Brandy (photograph © 1983 by Jill Krementz)

LEFT: *Associated Press photo
of Millar conferring with Los
Angeles police during search
for Linda*
(Wide World Photos)

RIGHT: *Millar in 1961*
(photo Ray Borges
Santa Barbara News-Press)

BELOW: *Covers for Fontana
paperback editions, 1970–1972*

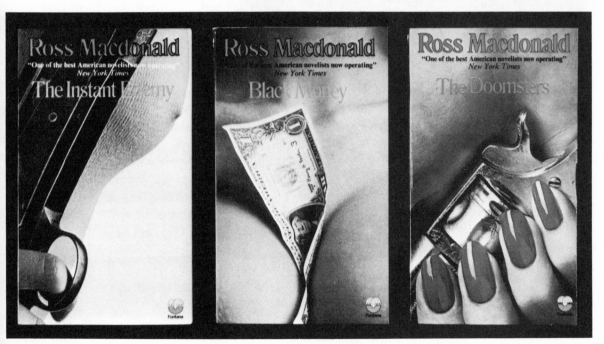

insulating point of view in *The Galton Case*, Millar dropped Archer in his next novel, partly because Knopf and his salesmen had been urging him to stop writing series mysteries. The reading public had not yet responded enthusiastically to Archer. *The Ferguson Affair* (1960)—originally titled "Death Mask" and "The Silver Dollar Tree"—is narrated by Bill Gunnarson, a California lawyer. He is drawn into the problems of Colonel Ferguson, a Canadian oil millionaire married to movie actress Holly May, young enough to be his daughter. Holly appears to have staged her own kidnapping, and her husband regards his troubles a condign punishment for having deserted a pregnant girl when he was at Harvard. There is an appalling point at which Ferguson appears to have married his own daughter; but Holly is actually the half sister of his corrupt daughter, who has been impersonating Holly and has arranged the kidnapping. There is no element of the child's search for a parent involved in the plot. Ferguson's natural daughter is a sociopath whose crimes are motivated by envy of her fortunate half sister. *The Ferguson Affair* explores the obverse of the Oedipus story—a parent's discovery of an exiled child from Laius's perspective.

As an expectant father, Gunnarson is able to sympathize with Ferguson, whose wife is also pregnant; but nothing particularly important for the novel is gained by substituting Gunnarson for Archer. One can only somewhat lamely conclude that again—as in *Meet Me at the Morgue*—Millar was demonstrating to himself and his readers that he was not dependent on Archer. Having made the point, he thereafter stayed with Archer, although he intended to bring back Gunnarson in a later book.

The Ferguson Affair was Knopf's most successful Ross Macdonald title to date, requiring three trade printings in 1960. The movies paid $16,500, but did not produce it. With this book Millar transferred to Collins as his English publisher and received a £1,000 advance for each of his next four novels. It was a good move because Collins published the popular Crime Club series in cloth and owned the Fontana paperback imprint. Some of Millar's subsequent paperback exposure and sales in England can probably be credited to the striking Fontana covers, which he disliked. The English take what they call "thrillers" more seriously than Americans do, and in the early sixties Millar's English readership steadily grew, though the critical reaction still lagged.

The Ferguson Affair was followed by seven Archer novels in nine years: *The Wycherly Woman* (1961), *The Zebra-Striped Hearse* (1962), *The Chill* (1964), *The Far Side of the Dollar* (1965), *Black Money* (1966), *The Instant Enemy* (1968), and *The Goodbye Look* (1969)— which was Millar's first best seller. This period, spanning Millar's forty-fifth to fifty-fourth years, was a time of consolidation and mastery. It could be claimed with little hyperbole that each novel improved on its predecessor. All explore the problems of paternity or identity in terms of the resurrected past. Despite common themes, each novel is fresh; there is no duplication of characters (except for Archer) or plot. However, there are certain recognizable character types: the homicidal female, the young loser-victim, the arrogant rich man.

These novels demonstrate an increasing virtuosity with plot reversal and the peeling away of layers of false identity. The effect of the plots is to provide the reader with a sense of participating in Archer's emerging revelations as he probes old crimes and their reverberations. There is a clear impression that the chronicle is finding its own resolutions required by the mechanism of the past. Although the endings are surprising and even shocking, the technique is thematically functional: "The surprise with which a detective novel concludes should set up tragic vibrations which run backward through the entire structure, which means that the structure must be single and *intended*."[21]

There are no tricks. The reader knows what Archer knows; only Archer's hunches are withheld. Indeed, there is a sense in which it is misleading to classify Millar as a suspense writer, in spite of the excitement provided by his resolutions. His concern is not whodunnit or how-he-dunnit, but why-he-dunnit (usually why-she-dunnit). To say that he writes novels of character is tautological because all good novels are novels of character; if the readers don't believe in the characters, they don't believe in the book. It was necessary for Millar to integrate character with the requirements of complex structures. Critics of the later novels have complained that the characters are creatures of plot, but Millar insisted that his characters shape the plots. "Action is character," as Fitzgerald noted.

Nonetheless, Millar's characters are not deeply probed or extensively developed. This disparity is not readily perceived because they are exposed —or expose themselves—in times of strain through dialogue, providing an impression of intensity. His condensed characterizations are mainly the result of the requirements of form—the novel of 250 to 280 pages. Packing a great deal of plot into this tight length provides the novels with a rapid pace. Finally, Millar may have been willing to skimp on character development because of his concern with the sociological determinism of Southern California—a land where many things begin and many things end. Although his stories sometimes have their seeds elsewhere, they could have blossomed only in California—where the cash crops are money and sex.

The plot interest of Millar's novels tends to distract attention from their social commentary. The subject of his criticism is not institutions or systems, but the effects of money on those who have it and those who want it: the arrogance of the rich and the yearning of the poor. He creates a population of self-destructive young losers, often the victims of traumatic childhoods. The greatest crime is to damage a child. Injustice grieves him; but Millar is not essentially concerned with the system of justice, which he views as an extension of the class structure. (Rich murderers never go to the gas chamber.) He remarked that his later work is less concerned with human justice than with divine justice: "The word 'divine' is not meant to bring theological assumptions, though it refers to a more inclusive reality than the human. I think my later novels are constructed to represent the workings of divine justice, that immensely complex causality which governs our lives and is influenced by our lives in turn, for they are part of it, even our secret and unconscious selves. . . . In my books causality is shown in the light of irony which I try to make tragic, that is, seriously concerned with human fate."[22]

Archer spends much of his working time driving up and down the coast; the highway and the ocean become incremental symbols. The highway represents the mobility and disjointedness of California life. Archer ruminates: "I had to admit to myself that I lived for nights like these, moving across the city's great broken body, making connections among its millions of cells. I had a crazy wish or fantasy that someday before I died, if I made all the right neural connections, the city would come all the way alive. Like the Bride of Frankenstein."[23]

The Pacific Ocean, to which Millar responded in terms of the pathetic fallacy, provides a changing expression of man's relationship with nature; it assumes the qualities of the people around it. Millar felt a strong affinity with the sea. One day he suggested to Robert Easton that they rent a sailboat. Since Millar seemed to know what he was doing, Easton was happy to crew for him while they sailed for several hours. At the end of the uneventful excursion Millar admitted that it was the first time he had tried to sail.

The Wycherly Woman (originally titled "The Basilisk Look") begins as a missing-daughter case but develops into a paternity problem. The missing Phoebe Wycherly—who has been impersonating her murdered mother, an unlikely twist—is actually the daughter of her putative uncle. Because he is dependent upon the Wycherly fortune, he has murdered Phoebe's mother to prevent exposure. At the end Archer assists divine justice by allowing the killer to commit suicide in order to protect Phoebe from courtroom disclosure of her paternity. The book was dedicated to Dorothy Olding. Reviewer James Sandoe was moved to rhetorical praise in the *New York Herald Tribune*: "How does one do justice to a tale that sets one in the rare state of fascinated absorption that we hope for and so rarely discover?"[24]

The Zebra-Striped Hearse studies the problem of concealed paternity in terms of an Electra figure. Wealthy Colonel Blackwell hires Archer to investigate the fiancé of his homely daughter, Harriet. The young man, Campion, is trying to solve the murder of his young wife, Dolly—a homicide that he suspects is connected with the Blackwells. It develops that Dolly had given birth to Colonel Blackwell's child and was murdered by Harriet Blackwell, who wanted Campion but also wanted to punish Dolly for taking her father from her. Among Millar's rejected titles for the novel were "The Whiteheaded Boy," "The Living Eye," "Murder Country," "The People Watcher," "The Blackwell Imbroglio," and "The Blackwell Tragedy."

Millar regarded *The Chill* as his strongest plot thus far, and it ends with one of his best reversals. Archer is hired to find a runaway bride, who as a child had witnessed the murder of her mother. The case involves the dean of the local college and his domineering wealthy mother. Another old murder in the Midwest is resurrected by a female instructor at the college, who is herself murdered. All the murders connect; all were committed by the dean's mother—who is actually his wife. Here Millar has invented a false oedipal story: The wife assumes the role of mother to her young hus-

Notes for The Zebra-Striped Hearse
(Special Collections, University Library, University of California, Irvine)

Notes for The Far Side of the Dollar
(Special Collections, University Library, University of California, Irvine)

band, who seeks to free himself from the relationship. The British Crime Writers' Association awarded its Silver Dagger to *The Chill* as runner-up for the best crime novel of the year.

Millar liked his next novel, *The Far Side of the Dollar* (1965), well enough to select it for inclusion in his *Great Stories of Suspense* (1974). In the introduction to the anthology, he described Archer as "less the hero of the novel than its mind, an unwilling judge who is forced to see that a murderer can be his own chief victim."[25] The manuscript was written in 109 days (1 November 1963 to 17 February 1964). As usual, Millar had difficulty deciding among possible titles. The first page of his notes for revision lists these titles: "The Black Yarn," "You'll Find Out on Judgment Day," "The Serpent's Tooth," "The Underside of the Weave," "A Taste of Fire," "The Time Binders," and "The Far Side of the Dollar." Other titles in the manuscript are "The Deep Dark Night," "The Black Hole of Calcutta," "The Sea and the Highway," and "The Brass Bed." The dedication page, which read "To Alfred," reaffirmed Millar's loyalty to Knopf.

The novel begins with a runaway-child case when Archer is hired to find Tom Hillman, a seventeen-year-old escapee from the Laguna Perdita School for disturbed children. Ralph Hillman, the boy's wealthy father, had put him there the week before because Tom had wrecked a stolen car and for another reason that Hillman refuses to reveal. (The withheld information is that Tom had reacted violently to the discovery of the concealment of his adoption.) They are a troubled family. Ralph Hillman, a former Navy captain, is a vain man disappointed in his son. Hillman's wife, Elaine, is a neurotic with a puritanical New England background. The case turns into a kidnapping-extortion when Hillman receives a demand for $25,000 in return for information about his son.

After Archer learns that Tom had been seen with a blonde "old enough to be his mother," he finds the woman, Carol Brown, dead (chapter nine). Her photo is recognized by a Hollywood agent who puts Archer in touch with Susanna Drew, a television producer who had befriended Carol during the war. (Conveniently, Susanna is Archer's old girl friend.) Susanna had helped her when Carol was left pregnant at the Barcelona Hotel in Santa Monica by Mike Harley, an AWOL sailor. Archer follows the trail to Las Vegas, where Mike has lost the $25,000 ransom in a poker game, and then to Pocatello and learns that Carol had put her baby up for adoption (chapter seventeen). At this point the trained Millar reader can predict what became of the baby.

Archer finds Harley dead at the Barcelona—where the story really began. Elaine Hillman reveals to Archer that Tom is adopted, a secret that had been kept from him (chapter twenty-one). Archer captures Tom—who has been holed up in the Barcelona—and takes him home. Hillman reveals that he is really Tom's father, having impregnated Carol at the Barcelona (chapter twenty-seven). At the same time he was having an affair with Susanna. Elaine was sterile as well as frigid, and Hillman wanted a son—partly to compensate for the massacre of his squadron at Midway. Unwilling to leave Elaine because he needed her money, Hillman had concealed Tom's parentage from her.

Elaine admits both murders. She had killed Carol after learning that she was Tom's mother, and Mike to conceal the first murder. Elaine asks Archer to let her take an overdose of sleeping pills. He refuses, and she commits suicide with her knitting needles (chapter twenty-eight).

The plot begins to work toward its resolution in chapter twenty-one when Elaine tells Archer that Tom was adopted, although she claims that her husband is the sterile partner. Exposing the past to Archer, Elaine remarks on "the deep connections you get in life, the coming together of the past and the present."[26] Seven chapters out of twenty-eight—one-quarter of the novel—are devoted to unraveling the truth about Tom's parentage and the murders.* It is a simplification to say that the extended resolution intensifies suspense, which is a by-product of Millar's peeling away the layered past. Archer comments in chapter fourteen, "It gave me the queer feeling that time was repeating itself and would go on endlessly repeating itself, as it does in hell."[27] He is discovering the meanings of the story, a process the reader is made to share. The events fulfill their own deterministic logic. Millar usually had more material than he could use, and the plot elements synthesized as he wrote: ". . . the over-all plot is generally in my mind, but the way I work it out has to be invented as I go; the *intention* of the book has to be worked out as I go."[28] In his notes for the novel there is the complication of a Nevada gangster who is Carol's lover, as well as a final shoot-out between Archer and Mike Harley.

The plotting of *The Far Side of the Dollar* is not flawless. Millar has a

* The manuscript has a twenty-ninth chapter, in which Archer and Susanna tentatively resume their relationship.

weakness for the lucky lead. Archer's discovery of the motel key that leads him to Carol is too easy. Susanna Drew's past relationship with both Archer and Hillman is too convenient. The first draft reveals that it was an afterthought to provide a past connection between Archer and Susanna; but Millar needed her to establish the lead to the Barcelona and the brass bed on which Tom was conceived.

George Grella has persuasively argued that Millar's later novels at times "seem to be about their plots." He has identified four congruent plots that form an organic structure: "The Quest of Archer, The Search for the Past, The Metamorphic Pattern and The Mythic Plot."[29] Thus, in *The Far Side of the Dollar* Archer is hired to find Tom Hillman, which immediately plunges him into the history of the Hillman family. But people and circumstances undergo a process of flux: Tom is/is not/is Hillman's son. The permutations of identity result in a mythlike effect, the impression of an archetypal allegory. As in most myths, action and place repeat themselves. Deception begets deception. Crime begets crime.

The reviews of *The Far Side of the Dollar* were the best yet. Boucher declared in the *New York Times Book Review*:

> Without in the least abating my admiration for Dashiell Hammett and Raymond Chandler, I should like to venture the heretical suggestion that Ross Macdonald is a better novelist than either of them. He owes an immeasurable debt to both in the matter of technique and style; but he has gone beyond their tutelage to develop the "hardboiled," private-eye novel into a far more supple medium, in which he can study the common and uncommon man (and woman) as well as the criminal, in which he can write (often brilliantly and even profoundly) not only about violence and retribution but simply about "people with enough feeling to be hurt, and enough complexity to do wrong"—to quote from his latest. . . .[30]

Knopf printed Boucher's review as an ad. In the *London Sunday Times* Symons expressed the wish that Millar would push beyond the Chandler framework, noting aspects of the novel, "like the increased play given to Archer's evangelism, which suggest that Mr. Macdonald's talent may still be capable of development."[31] The Crime Writers' Association awarded *The Far Side of the Dollar* its Golden Dagger; and in 1965 Millar was elected president of the Mystery Writers of America, an honorary position. In his presidential statement he wrote:

> I thank you for the very special honor, which I won't deny I've aspired to, the more intensely in the years since Margaret Millar was elected President of MWA.
>
> My memory wanders much further back to the high school days when my distinguished predecessor and I were always bumping into each other in the stacks of the Kitchener (Ontario) Public Library. We were preparing ourselves for a life of crime by reading our way through the mystery section, a category which the librarian (Miss Mabel Dunham, a novelist in her own right) interpreted loosely. I had read all of *Crime and Punishment* before I realized that I had been conned by an expert.
>
> There may be a point, after all, in this not very pointed reminiscence. As custodians of the mystery tradition in America, I think we should interpret its limits loosely and with a certain pride and hopefulness. While there may not be a Dostoevsky among us, our craft has provided the matrix for some of the classics of our literature.
>
> Under the pressure of publishers' deadlines and bills that have to be paid, it isn't easy to try and write for some word-happy kid haunting a provincial library who might just possibly find in our work a viable tradition, native as jazz, complex in potential as Elizabethan drama. But if we write with an eye to that possibility, we may stumble into some new excellence.[32]

The success of the *Harper* movie (from *The Moving Target*) made Millar a hot writer and generated interest in his out-of-print books, which Bantam began republishing with the cover slug: "Lew Archer—the hardest of the hard-boiled dicks." He received more scripting offers than he could handle; in 1966 he worked on a screenplay for *Blue City*, prepared a presentation for a television series about a husband-and-wife detective team, and tried to provide plot for a plotless movie being shot in Hong Kong and London. None of these projects came to anything. Millar told Herbert Harker, "A movie isn't the best thing that can happen to a writer. It changes his work, and it changes him."[33] These changes are not detectable in his own novels after *Harper*; there is no indication that Millar

LEFT: *Movie tie-in edition of* The Moving Target, *1966*

BELOW: *Lobby still,* Harper, *1966*

began writing with an eye toward movie sales. Indeed, in 1966 he turned down a $35,000 movie deal for *The Chill* because the studio didn't want to retain Archer.

Millar regarded his nineteenth novel, *Black Money* (1966), as probably his strongest work; it "seems to have a tone I don't have anywhere else."[34] He had been planning to write it for a long time, but had postponed it. When he got down to work, he wrote it with the blinds drawn. The rejected titles included "The Darkness at the Window," "The Scrambling Shadow," and "The Demon Lover" (which was the title for the *Cosmopolitan* condensation). His fullest acknowledgment of F. Scott Fitzgerald —"my dream writer"[35]—*Black Money* is a sixties California version of *The Great Gatsby*. Archer is hired to investigate the background of Francis Martel, a wealthy Frenchman who has married a local girl named Ginny Fablon. Martel proves to be Pedro Domingo, AKA Feliz Cervantes, the son of a Panama bar girl. As courier for a Nevada gambler, he has stolen black money (undeclared cash) in order to marry Ginny. But his Daisy is even more corrupt than Gatsby's. Ginny married Martel to obtain money to run off with her lover, a failed professor of French. In the end Domingo/Cervantes/Martel, like Gatz Gatsby, is killed by his pursuit of the American Dream Girl. *Black Money* has the final appearance of a gangster in the series; thereafter Millar confined himself to domestic criminals and family tragedies.

The scholarly pursuits of Ginny's lover provided Millar with an opportunity for academic parody, as though to reassure himself that he was well out of that game. Tappinger is one of those professors with a "major book" in progress that will never be written. Here is the opening of his study of the French influences on Crane:

Stephen Crane lived like a god in the adamantine city of the mind. Where did he find the prototype of that city? In Athens the marmoreal exemplar of the West, or in the supernal blueprint which Augustine bequeathed to us in his *Civitas Dei*? Or was it in Paris the City of Art? Perchance he looked on his whore's body with the massive cold pity of Manet's *Olympe*. Perhaps the luminous city of his mind was delved from the mud of Cora's loins.[36]

Lew Archer saved Kenneth Millar from twenty years of that.

Notes for Black Money (Special
Collections, University Library,
University of California, Irvine)

New York Times Book Review,
1 May 1966

This dossier of the great
Lew Archer cases marks
the ones still in print
with a dagger.†
(With luck you can track the rest
down on a collector's shelf.)

THE MOVING TARGET
(1949)

THE DROWNING POOL
(1950)

THE WAY SOME
PEOPLE DIE
(1951)

THE IVORY GRIN
(1952)

FIND A VICTIM
(1954)

THE BARBAROUS COAST
(1956)

THE DOOMSTERS
(1958)

†THE GALTON CASE
(1959, $3.00)

†THE WYCHERLY
WOMAN
(1961, $3.50)

†THE ZEBRA-STRIPED
HEARSE
(1962, $3.50)

†THE CHILL
(1964, $3.95)

†THE FAR SIDE OF
THE DOLLAR
(1965, $3.95)

*And testing Archer to his
astonishing limits, the latest
and best case*

The Case for
ROSS
MACDONALD
(Just for the record—
13 perfect crimes)

Photo: Alfred A. Knopf

BLACK
MONEY
$3.95
Now at better bookstores

I T'S no secret to connoisseurs of
crime-in-print that Macdonald's
master of detection, Lew Archer, has
just unsnarled his 13th—and by all odds,
strangest—case, BLACK MONEY. And
unsnarled it in bravura Archer form.

A circumstance that led Anthony
Boucher to comment immediately in
the *New York Times*, "There's one
prediction a reviewer can safely venture in any January; that Macdonald's
annual Lew Archer story will be the
best private-eye novel of the year."

Fact is, in 17 years of making murder, mayhem, and the darker side of
human nature his business, Macdonald
has never turned in a dull performance.
Lesser men keep a sharp lookout for
the legal loophole or the damning fin-
gerprint. Macdonald goes to the heart
of the crime. And the criminal.

The blood was spilled in Archer's
first case, *The Moving Target*, in 1949
when Macdonald was young and unknown. (And is being spilled with fascinating results again in *Harper*, a new
Warner Bros. movie based on *The
Moving Target*, with Paul Newman
playing Archer.) Happily for the
aficionado, Macdonald has been plotting complex crimes ever since for
Archer to get to the bottom of. Cur-
rently president of the Mystery Writers
of America, Macdonald has staked
claim to his native California as the
gilded backdrop for his mysteries.

"Thinking man's mysteries", Virginia
Kirkus calls them. Which is something
other critics have been quick to note.
Viz.

"Ross Macdonald should not be limited
in audience to connoisseurs of mystery
fiction. He is one of a handful of writers in the genre whose worth and
quality surpass the limitations of the
form."
— ROBERT KIRSCH,
Los Angeles Times

"Ross Macdonald is an important
American novelist."—WILLIAM HOGAN,
San Francisco Chronicle

"Ross Macdonald has become the best
writer we have about California and
one of the country's best novelists."
— ROGER SALE, *Argus*

"Without in the least abating my admiration for Dashiell Hammett and
Raymond Chandler, I should like to
venture the heretical suggestion that
Macdonald is a better novelist than
either of them." — ANTHONY BOUCHER,
New York Times Book Review

ALFRED · A · KNOPF

During 1960 Millar had made an effort to publish his Coleridge dissertation, which he had revised with the help of Donald Davie. It was declined by Harvard, Cassell, Knopf, Routledge, Indiana University, and Oxford. He was stung by the outside reader's report from Harvard that said he had failed to make use of recent developments in Coleridge scholarship. Millar planned to update the references but gave up on it, saying that the experience had confirmed the wisdom of his decision to leave the academic life.

In 1967 Knopf published *Archer in Hollywood*, the first of three Archer omnibus volumes, followed by *Archer at Large* (1970) and *Archer in Jeopardy* (1979). It was Millar's idea to collect *The Moving Target*, *The Way Some People Die*, and *The Barbarous Coast* because they hadn't sold well when originally published. The title *Archer in Hollywood* was misleading: except for *The Barbarous Coast*, the novels have very little to do with Hollywood. His foreword concluded: "We writers, as we work our way deeper into our craft, learn to drop more and more personal clues. Like burglars who secretly wish to be caught, we leave our fingerprints on the broken locks, our voiceprints in the bugged rooms, our footprints in the wet concrete and the blowing sand."

The Instant Enemy (1968), Millar's most intricately plotted novel, involves an identity quest through three generations of imposture. Seventeen-year-old Sandy Sebastian has run off with a nineteen-year-old loser, Davy Spanner. Archer's first meeting with Sandy elicits a remarkable description: "Her body thrust itself forward and leaned on Davy's with the kind of heartbroken lewdness that only very young girls are capable of."[37] It is later revealed that she had been drugged and raped by Stephen Hackett, the wealthy employer of her father. Sandy and Davy abduct Hackett. Archer's first sight of the Hackett estate at Malibu employs imagery to alert the attentive reader: "Quail were calling in the brush, and smaller birds were eating red berries off the toyon. A couple of soaring vultures balanced high on a thermal were keeping an eye on things."[38] The setting seems pastoral; but the vultures are waiting for carrion.

As a child Davy had been found by the side of a railroad track next to the decapitated body of his father. The body was never identified; Davy is trying to find out who he is and who murdered his father. As Archer traces Davy's past, he observes: "Coincidences seldom happen in my work. If you dig deep enough, you can nearly always find their single bifurcating roots."[39] This working rule is reinforced three pages later by a strong image of sexual corruption: "This case was opening, not like a door or even a grave, certainly not like a rose or any other flower, but opening like an old sad blonde with darkness at her core."[40]

The plot culminates in a double reversal, which Archer foreshadows in terms of Stephen Hackett's Klee: "It showed a man in a geometrical maze, and seemed to show that the man and the maze were continuous with each other."[41] Stephen Hackett is really Jasper Blevins, who murdered his half brother Stephen and assumed his identity to gain control of the Hackett fortune. Davy Spanner is the out-of-wedlock son of the actual Stephen Hackett. Along the way Jasper committed three other murders in collusion with his mother—who is Stephen's mother and Davy's grandmother.

The Hacketts have paid Archer with a postdated $100,000 check, conditional on his covering up for them. The concluding words of the novel are: "I tore it into small pieces and tossed the yellow confetti out the window. It drifted down on the short hairs and the long hairs, the potheads and the acid heads, draft dodgers and dollar chasers, swingers and walking wounded, idiot saints, hard cases, foolish virgins."

In a 1967 interview Millar commented that at one time Margaret objected to the hard-boiled line he was taking: "I didn't take it; it took me. It was a reaction to the war, a substitute for a postwar nervous breakdown. I think very few people are aware of the enormous erosion of sensibility that war causes, and the enormous changes in the quality of a civilization that it brings about. I'm out of that particular period now, but someday I'd like to write something which didn't come from the damned war."[42] Although he never wrote about battle, the aftereffects of World War II reverberate throughout much of Millar's fiction. *The Far Side of the Dollar*, in which present time is the sixties, is about war casualties. At the time of this interview he was working on *The Goodbye Look*, a novel he intended to call "The Stolen War." Millar explained that the "original intent of the novel was anti-war" and that he had "drained off some of the sorrow of this national moment into it."[43]

In 1968 Millar declined a bid to write the screenplay for a remake of *The Maltese Falcon*. The death of Anthony Boucher that year deprived him of his most trusted critic.

~~ FOUR ~~

The Goodbye Look (1969), Millar's twenty-first novel, provided his popular and critical breakthrough when he was fifty-three. He described it as "the one least likely to have been written by anyone else."[1] Though no stronger than his previous four novels, it was the one that caught on. Before the book was published, Knopf editors Ashbel Green and Robert Gottlieb had lunch with John Leonard, the editor of the *New York Times Book Review*; they told Leonard that something ought to be done to get Millar off the capsule mystery review page. William Goldman's front-page review in the *New York Times Book Review* was headlined "The finest detective novels ever written by an American."* (Goldman had written the screenplay for *Harper*.) Millar's time had come—a bit late, as is often the

* This statement was quoted on the front covers of Millar's subsequent Bantam paperbacks. Goldman actually wrote: "the finest series of detective novels ever written by an American."

case with a popular writer crossing the border to respectability. Goldman claimed that "Macdonald's work in the last decade has nothing remotely to do with hard-boiled detective novels. He is writing novels of character about people with ghosts."[2] It would have been more accurate to say that he had adapted the conventions of hard-boiled detective fiction for his identity-quest novels. Goldman's review was reinforced by Leonard's interview with Millar, which noted, "Ten years ago [with *The Galton Case*] while nobody was watching—or, rather, while everyone was looking in the wrong direction—a writer of detective stories turned into a major American novelist."[3] *Newsweek* and *Time* published tardy reviews. *Newsweek* made the point that it was time to reassess Millar without reference to the hard-boiled school: *The Goodbye Look* "confirms Macdonald's metamorphosis from an imitator of Dashiell Hammett and Raymond Chandler into a novelist who uses the detective tradition to explore the modern American psyche."[4] But *Time* complained that Millar had become a pompous pontificator; and the *New Yorker* said that his characters had become predictable.

In *The Goodbye Look* Archer's assignment to recover a stolen gold box leads to a concealed paternity and concealed identity plot almost as complex as that of *The Instant Enemy*. The box—which the novel identifies with Pandora's box—belongs to a fortunate couple, the wealthy war hero Lawrence Chalmers and his beautiful wife, Irene. Their troubled twenty-three-year-old son, Nick, is implicated in the theft. Archer traces the box to Jean Swain, a middle-aged woman searching for her lost father, the embezzler Eldon Swain, who ran off with Rita Shepherd twenty-four years before. Swain was robbed by Lawrence Chalmers and Rita Shepherd (who was pregnant with Swain's child, Nick) ; Rita is Irene Chalmers. The bogus war hero, Chalmers, has committed three murders to conceal his past—as well as having caused his mother's death and having attempted to murder Nick. Exposed, Chalmers puts on a Navy commander's uniform and cuts his throat.

Although the reversals are effective, the plotting seems unnecessarily —even arbitrarily—complicated. After Chalmers and Rita rob Swain, they implausibly commit a reverse burglary by hiding the half-million dollars in his mother's house. And there is at least one loose end. It is established that when Nick was eight, he murdered his natural father, Eldon Swain, who had abducted him. Fifteen years later the revolver that killed Swain is used by Chalmers to commit another murder; but there is no explanation of how it came into his possession.

Archer has developed the need to account for himself: " 'I have a secret passion for mercy. . . . But justice is what keeps happening to people.' "[5] And: "But if I started to use the woman and the occasion, I'd be using a part of myself and my life that I tried to keep unused: the part that made the difference between me and a computer, or a spy."[6] Explaining his way of life, Archer says, " 'When your income passes a certain point you lose touch. All of a sudden the other people look like geeks or gooks, expendables.' "[7]

The Goodbye Look was on the *Times* best seller list for fourteen weeks, reaching number seven. None of Millar's previous novels had sold more than 10,000 copies in cloth. The Knopf edition went through eight printings between May and October, and the novel was a Mystery Guild selection. Beginning with *The Goodbye Look*, the Knopf dust jackets announced "The New Lew Archer Novel"—marketing him as a brand name. Bantam initiated a program to reprint all of Millar's books in paperback, and the results were probably better than anticipated: between 1969 and 1976 there were more than 125 Bantam printings. In 1971 Millar's total sales passed 5 million copies.* At the same time he became a world author; incomplete figures show that by 1969 he sold 859,000 copies in Italy, 418,000 in France, and 200,000 in Germany. Millar had always sought to write what he regarded as a democratic novel—a serious novel in a popular genre—and his paperbacks reached the audience he wanted. "The idea to do what I do came partly from the blues. It was the idea of a popular art that would give a picture of society to the society."[8] Millar had a collection of jazz records, and Duke Ellington was his favorite composer. Such comparisons are always approximate, but it might be said that Millar's prose has an Ellingtonian sophistication rather than, say, the vigor of Jelly Roll Morton.

Millar's fame brought many requests for interviews, about which he was generously cooperative, despite his reserve. He did not enjoy being a celebrity, but was too kind to refuse people who wanted his help. The

---

* Millar was still something of a gourmet writer in a junk-food supermarket. Spillane's books had sold some 100 million copies.

Alfred A. Knopf, Ashbel Green, and Millar
(photograph © 1983 by Jill Krementz)

RIGHT: *Trial titles for* The Goodbye Look *(Special Collections, University Library, University of California, Irvine)*

BELOW: New York Times Book Review, *22 June 1969*

BELOW RIGHT: *Jacket for Millar's first best-seller, 1969*

OPPOSITE: *Millar at the height of success* (photograph © 1983 by Jill Krementz)

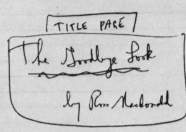

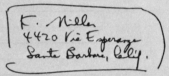

The New York Times
has just called the novels of

Ross Macdonald

"the finest detective novels
ever written by an American."

His new one is

The Goodbye Look

It has just arrived
at bookstores all over the
country. Price $4.95.
Buy it now. (*Ada* can wait.)

The front page review in *The Times Book Review* concludes: "Classify him as you will, he is one of the best American novelists now operating, and all he does is keep on getting better."

And you will probably want a check list of his other books. Here they are — most of them in print in the Knopf editions or in paperback.

THE INSTANT ENEMY (1968)
ARCHER IN HOLLYWOOD (1967) *an omnibus containing*
  THE MOVING TARGET
  THE WAY SOME PEOPLE DIE
  THE BARBAROUS COAST
BLACK MONEY (1966)
THE FAR SIDE OF THE DOLLAR (1965)
THE CHILL (1964)
THE ZEBRA-STRIPED HEARSE (1962)

THE WYCHERLY WOMAN (1961)
THE FERGUSON AFFAIR (1960)
THE GALTON CASE (1959)
THE DOOMSTERS (1958)
THE BARBAROUS COAST (1956)
FIND A VICTIM (1954)
MEET ME AT THE MORGUE (1953)
THE IVORY GRIN (1952)
THE WAY SOME PEOPLE DIE (1951)
THE DROWNING POOL (1950)
THE MOVING TARGET (1949)

Alfred · A · Knopf

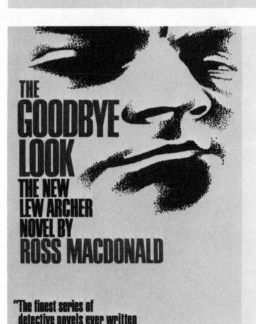

THE
GOODBYE
LOOK
THE NEW
LEW ARCHER
NOVEL BY
ROSS MACDONALD

"The finest series of
detective novels ever written
by an American."
William Goldman on *The Goodbye Look*
in *The New York Times Book Review*

Millar in the late 1960s (photograph © 1983 by Jill Krementz)

interviewers often mentioned Millar's shy, diffident gaze and his soft, thrifty speech, which retained a faint Scottish-Canadian burr. (William Campbell Gault has described his smile as a combination of Gioconda and Stan Laurel.) He spoke and moved deliberately. Once when he was performing a household chore, Margaret told him to hurry up. "When you hurry, you bump into things," he replied. Millar's friends claim that he was capable of spending hours in their company without saying much between hello and goodbye. "I'm a naturally depressed person," he insisted. Yet he was moved to angry speech by political issues; Barry Goldwater, Richard Nixon, and Ronald Reagan were reliable triggers. His convictions were unshakable, and he broke off friendships when he found that a friend's principles were contrary to his own. Robert Easton sensed that Millar "seethed with restrained violence."[9]

Linda Millar Pagnusat died at thirty-one in November 1970, leaving a husband and son. Millar wrote Dorothy Olding: "The people who knew her best, including her husband and me, felt that she was in almost unaccountable ways a great person. . . . Like my mother, her great ambition was to look after the sick, and in fact she was looking for work in that field the day she died."[10]

In 1964 the Coyote Canyon fire had come within 200 or 300 yards of the Millar house; after the area had been evacuated, Millar had remained behind for two days hosing the roof. The first words he wrote in his notebook for *The Underground Man* (1971) in late summer 1969 were "An Ecological Crime." A fire in Santa Teresa symbolizes the interior fires that consume the characters. The meaning of "ecological" expands to include moral as well as environmental relationships, which overlap: "He belonged to a generation whose elders had been poisoned, like the pelicans, with a kind of moral DDT that damaged the lives of their young."[11] A pattern of war imagery runs through the novel, as though nature has been transmogrified into a human battlefield: "Darkening fruit hung down from their branches like green hand grenades."[12] Millar has remarked that crime is an extension of war.

Again, the novel begins as a father quest, and the fire is started by the cigarillo of Stanley Broadhurst, who is murdered while digging for the body of his murdered father. The third generation of Broadhursts is represented by Stanley's abducted son, Ronny, who arouses Archer's paternal feelings. Ronny is a portrait of Millar's grandson, Jimmy, "the only one I

Working draft for first page of The Underground Man *(Special Collections, University Library, University of California, Irvine)*

Jacket for Millar's second successive best-seller, 1971

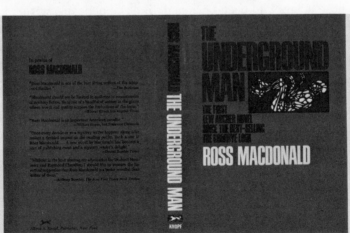

have ever drawn from life."[13] Millar repeats a favorite oedipal idea from *The Galton Case*: Stanley Broadhurst is "angry at his father for abandoning him; at the same time he misses him and loves him."[14] An ironic message is planted in the novel in the form of a letter written to Stanley by a minister: "The past can do very little for us—no more than it has already done, for good or ill—except in the end to release us. We must seek and accept release, and give release."[15] Neither Millar's characters nor Millar can accept this sound advice. The past is unreleasable; release from it usually comes in the form of death.

Archer is older and tired. Other people's tragedies have wearied him. He was thirty-five years old in *The Moving Target* (1949), so he would be fifty-six (roughly Millar's age) in *The Underground Man*. But Archer seems to stop at about fifty years. Even so, he does age; most fictional private eyes ignore the calendar.

Before *The Underground Man* was published, Millar informed Ashbel Green: "There is always moral pain involved in following a great success, and I never worked so hard on a book in my life. The main thing is that it's different from the others, from all the others indeed, and not a self-imitation. Looking over it in some coolness, I think it may get me some new readers. The nature of the action, fire and flight, brings the energy up to the surface and should make it more readily available to the ordinary reader. Not that I expect a further breakthrough in sales. But don't you think the breakthrough was not so much that of *Goodbye Look* (hardly my best book) but of the series? Having said that, let me add that I'm now inclined to write my first non-series book in ten years. But not right away."[16] As it turned out, not ever.

The success of *The Goodbye Look* was consolidated by *The Underground Man*, which brought a *Newsweek* cover story by Raymond Sokolov. The profile closed with characteristic Millar imagery: " 'One writes on a curve, on the backs of torn-off calendar sheets. A writer in his 50's will not recapture the blaze of youth, or the steadier passion that comes like a second and saner youth in his 40's if he's lucky. But he can lie in wait in his room—it must be at least the hundredth room by now—and keep open his imagination and the bowels of his compassion against the day when another book will haunt him like a ghost riding out of both the past and the future.' "[17]

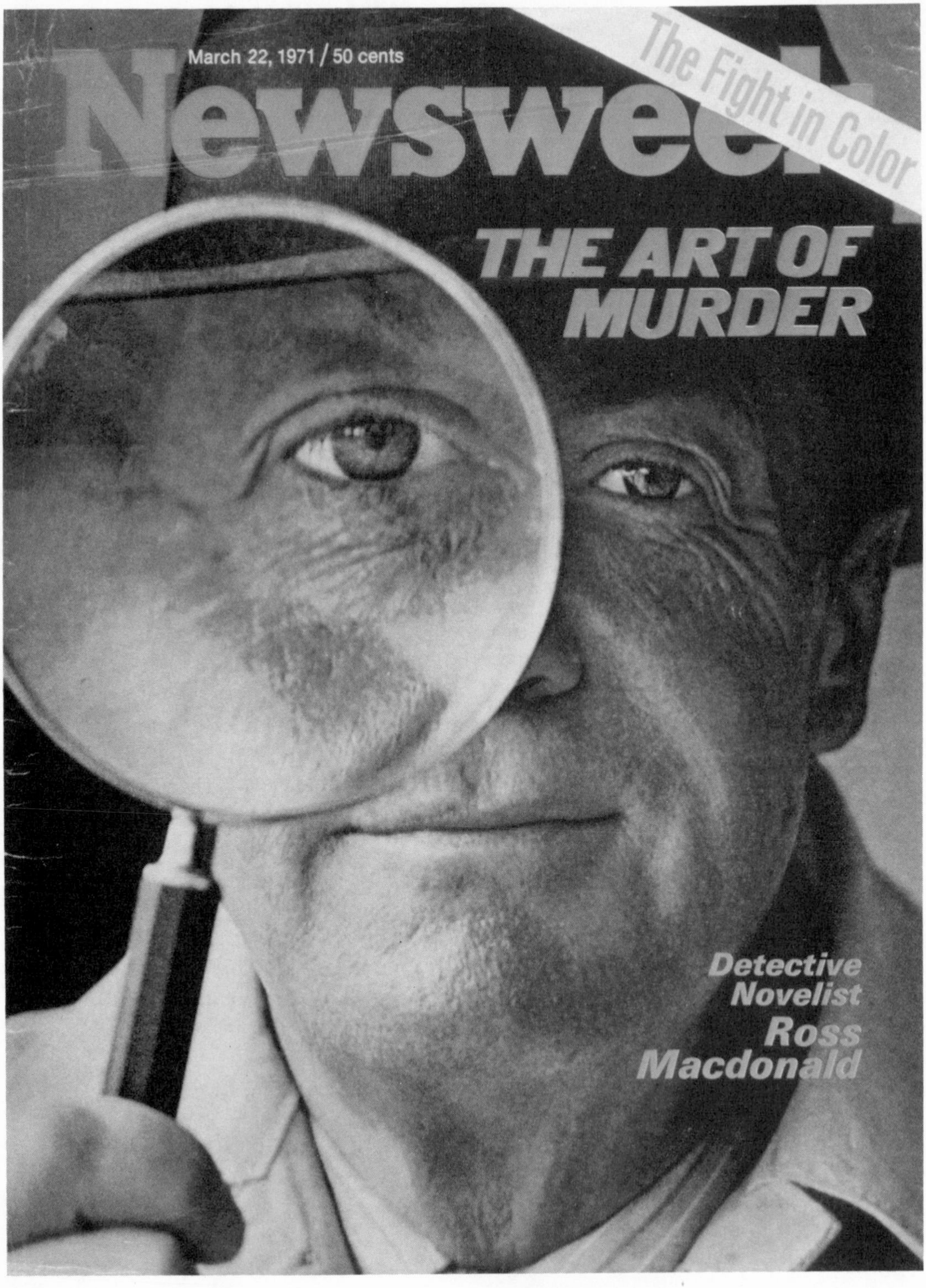
March 22, 1971 / 50 cents
Newsweek
The Fight in Color
THE ART OF MURDER
Detective Novelist Ross Macdonald

OPPOSITE: Newsweek *cover, 22 March 1971*
(Copyright 1971, by Newsweek, Inc. All
rights reserved. Reprinted by permission.)

ABOVE: *Millar with Eudora Welty*

RIGHT: *The* New York Times, *6 May 1974*

Eudora Welty's long review of *The Underground Man* received front-page treatment in the *New York Times Book Review*. Identifying it as his best novel, she noted the change in Archer from early cynicism to his present vulnerability: "He is at heart a champion, but a self-questioning, often a self-deriding champion. He is of today, one of ours. . . . In our day it is for such a novel as *The Underground Man* that the detective form exists."[18] At this time Millar and Miss Welty had not met. He greatly admired her writing and was moved by her appreciation of his work. After her review appeared, he introduced himself to Miss Welty in an elevator at the Algonquin Hotel in New York. They became warm friends, dedicating books to each other.

Launched by this exposure, *The Underground Man* became Millar's best-selling book. The first printing sold out before publication day, and there were five more Knopf printings—one of which was distributed by the Book-of-the-Month Club. The novel was on the *New York Times* best seller list for seventeen weeks, reaching number four, and sold 54,000 copies in the first six months. In 1974 it was made into a television movie.

The praise was not unanimous. Literary success usually begets counterreaction. A 1971 assessment of the Millar canon by Bruce Cook in the *New Catholic World* called *The Underground Man* a failure and his worst novel. Cook cited coincidences, plot flaws, weak motivation, and a resolution that requires the reader to believe that the eight people present at the murder scene have kept quiet for fifteen years.[19] Early in the novel Archer reiterates, "I don't believe in coincidences." This case—like others—builds from a lucky find that sets up a chain of connections. A runaway girl leaves behind a copy of *Green Mansions* with the names of two key plot figures written in it. Perhaps there are no accidents, either, in Archer's world. Clues are left by people who secretly want to be stopped.

Cook's reservations were shared by Richard Schickel in *Commentary*, who stated that Millar's reputation was "in process of gross inflation." Schickel cited a "stock company" of familiar characters and placed Millar's work in the escapist tradition embraced by Auden: "Whatever else work within the limits of this sort may be, however enthusiastically addicted to it we may become, it is not art—it is fantasy."[20]

The phrase "underground man" is a key Millar metaphor, going back to *The Three Roads* (1948). In his notebooks Millar observed:

The movement of the story could be described as the central character's gradual discovery that he is an underground man, to put it mildly.

What do I mean by an underground man? A character who represents the author, perhaps, but is given no special indulgence; who reflects a lack of interest in, even an impatience with special privilege —a sense of interdependence among men—a certain modesty. The central vice of the traditional hero, who easily accepts his own superiority, is hubris, an overweaning pride and expectation. The central vice of the underground *accidie*, moral and social sloth, a willingness to live with whatever is, a molelike inclination to accept the darkness. Perhaps these are the respective vices of aristocracy and democracy.

Among the classless men of our democracy the private detective has become a representative figure.[21]

Millar is obviously thinking with his fingers in this undated notebook entry, moving toward an analysis of the private detective's role as social saga hero.

The title of *The Underground Man* fortuitously accommodated itself to the buried murder victim, Leo Broadhurst. Millar's working title was "Digger"—meaning death. (Other rejected titles were "Rattlesnake," "Wildfire," "Where the Body Was Buried," "The Dissolving Man," "The Dying Animal," "The Warm Body," "The Bogey Man," and "The Burial Party.") The true underground man of the Millar canon is Lew Archer/Ross Macdonald/Kenneth Millar: "At its very best, where it grazes tragedy and transcends its own conventions, detective fiction can remind us that we are all underground men making a brief transit from darkness to darkness."[22] As an underground man Kenneth Millar hides in his novels but wants to be exhumed. Even without the aid of biographical research, the attentive reader of Millar's fiction is able to detect the recurring clues to the writer's unforgiven childhood and, later, to his own troubled child.

Millar's ruminations on the underground-man concept suggest another partly hidden aspect of his work: the tension between the aristocracy of literature and the democracy of subject. In 1977 he responded to the question "Who is the living writer you most admire?" by naming Nelson Algren: "The intensity of his feeling, the accuracy of his thought make me wonder if any other writer of our time has shown us more exactly the human basis of our democracy."[23] A self-described radical by reason of his childhood, Millar tried to democratize his fiction, to make it accessible to the common reader by choosing a popular genre. But art is hubristic. Culture erects barriers. His novels appeal to two distinct classes: those readers who recognize the permutations of the Oedipus myth as well as those who do not and don't care. Millar served both audiences without developing artistic schizophrenia. When his great success came, it had been prepared for by the people who read and write literary criticism as well as by the readers who bought the latest Lew Archer paperback. Indeed, he provided the lit-crit types with the snobbish satisfaction of being able to identify the sophistication in a mass-audience literature.

After *The Underground Man* Millar began thinking about writing a family and personal history, but decided that it was too soon "to embrace all that old sadness, the substance of my mother, the shadow of my father."[24]

His twenty-third novel, *Sleeping Beauty* (1973), explored the ramifications of another ecological crime. He and Margaret had been very active in the protests against the 1969 Santa Barbara oil spill; as a founder of GOO (Get Oil Out), Millar lent his name and pen to the cause.* The Millars were among the group who picketed Stearns Wharf, which was used by the oil rig crews. With Easton he established the Santa Barbara Citizens for Environmental Defense, to provide legal and scientific aid for people opposing the oil companies. Millar was gratified when he learned that his prepared *New York Times* obituary described him as a "novelist and environmentalist." He also took an active role in the Santa Barbara Citizens Commission on Civil Disorders, which prepared a report (much of it written by Millar) on the 1970 Isla Vista student riots. He opposed the Vietnam War but was not a pacifist, believing that war was justified against madmen such as Hitler.

The central symbol of *Sleeping Beauty* is an oil spill at Pacific Point; but it is a background symbol and does not directly influence the action, as the Santa Teresa fire did in *The Underground Man*. In the second paragraph Archer looks at the despoiled Pacific from a plane window: "An

---

* "Life with the Blob," *Sports Illustrated*, 21 April 1969, pp. 50–52; with Robert Easton, "Santa Barbarans Cite an 11th Commandment: 'Thou Shalt Not Abuse the Earth,' " *New York Times Magazine*, 12 October 1969, pp. 32–33, 142–149, 151, 156; and the Introduction to Robert Easton's *Black Tide* (New York: Delacorte, 1972).

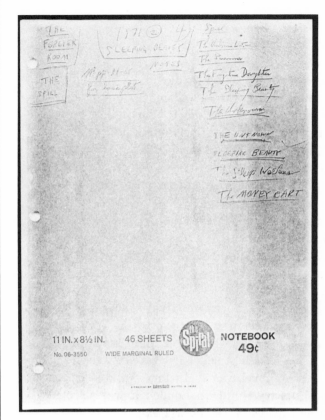

Notebook cover for Sleeping Beauty
(Special Collections, University Library,
University of California, Irvine)

Millar (right) *at Stearns Wharf, 1969*
(photo Bob Ponce, *Santa Barbara
News-Press*)

offshore oil platform stood up out of its windward end like the metal handle of a dagger that had stabbed the world and made it spill black blood." The rejected titles for *Sleeping Beauty* included "The Spill," "Spill," "The Forever Room," "The Survivor," "The Fugitive Daughter," "The Unknown," "The Sleep Walkers," and "The Money Cart." The plot is again generational, exposing concealed crimes as Archer traces the missing heiress of the family that owns the well. Verily, "The fathers have eaten a sour grape, and the children's teeth are set on edge."

The structure is again based on reduplicated action. The oil spill repeats a fuel gas spill on an aircraft carrier in 1945, and a twenty-five-year-old murder triggers more murders. But the plot loses track of the missing girl: she returns of her own accord, and it is lamely explained that she has been "wandering around."

Although *Sleeping Beauty* lacked the force of Millar's novels in the sixties, it was a commercial success. The first Knopf printing of 35,000 copies sold out before publication, and there were three more trade printings. It appeared on the *New York Times* best seller list for six weeks, but got no higher than number nine. The novel was a Mystery Guild selection and was also distributed by the Literary Guild. In London it was selected by Book Club Associates. But this time the *New York Times Book Review* turned sour on him. Crawford Woods contended that Millar had become the victim of his reputation, charging him with "careless detail work" and "literary pretension."[25] Millar wrote a rebuttal for the *Times*—the only time he publicly replied to a review:

Crawford Woods's review of my novel "Sleeping Beauty" contains three grotesque distortions. In each case, the distortion is accomplished with a thimblerigged quotation—and total suppression of its context.

(1) Woods picks up my sentence, "He was a tall dark man with a face that had known pain," and comments: "Lew Archer [my narrator] would find that gross as a description of a suspect. Why does the author settle for it as a portrait of a character?" But I don't. That single sentence is followed by a more exact descriptive sentence, then by an eight-page scene in which the "dark man" is the central character and his portrait is continually added to.

(2) Your reviewer states that my novel "crawls with spurious eschatology attached to un-fraught acts. When Archer takes an elevator

ride, he feels 'as if I were going down to the bottom of things.' " Woods delicately omits the fact that Archer's elevator is taking him to the morgue. A touch of the eschatological (does Woods realize it concerns death and other final matters?) is hardly out of place here.

(3) As evidence that Archer is "soggy with half-chewed California Zen," Woods quotes (or, rather, misquotes) the following passage: "If you drew your spirit deep into yourself and out of sight, it couldn't be destroyed. But it might go blind in the internal darkness." Deprived of their context, these sentences suggest that Archer is indulging in a self-centered philosophical solo. Actually, he is imagining the life of a woman he is interviewing. The whole passage reads as follows:

"Shock struck her face a glancing blow. I guessed that she had been struck that way many times before, and had learned the tricks of moral evasion. If you withdrew your spirit deep into yourself and out of sight, it couldn't be completely destroyed. But it might go blind in the internal darkness."

I have quoted this twice-mishandled paragraph in full to illustrate Woods's basic unfairness. Above all, to show exactly how his phony gloss makes Archer seem pretentious. And how, at the same time, he has used that gloss to drain the passage of its meaning.[26]

An unsigned review in the *New Republic* also charged that Millar's reputation was inflated—citing him for "a weakness for phony profundities," "a gross appetite for fancy imagery," and "a penchant for howlingly improbable pulp-psychology."[27]

In 1973 Millar worked on an ending for Dickens's *The Mystery of Edwin Drood* for the Canadian Broadcasting Corporation, but the project was canceled. NBC television launched *Archer*, in January 1975, with Brian Keith in the title role. The show was discontinued after seven weeks. Millar did not write the scripts.

Knopf published Millar's anthology *Great Stories of Suspense* in 1974.* His introduction acknowledged that he had learned his craft from

* The 800-page volume includes five novels: Agatha Christie's *What Mrs. McGuillicuddy Saw!*, Kenneth Fearing's *The Big Clock*, Robert Louis Stevenson's *The Strange Case of Dr. Jekyll and Mr. Hyde*, Dick Francis's *Enquiry*, and Millar's *The Far Side of the Dollar*. Among the short stories are Hammett's "Flypaper," Cain's "The Baby in the Icebox," and Margaret Millar's "The Couple Next Door." Chandler was not represented.

Hammett, Chandler, and Cain. After differentiating between the pure detective story (what has happened) and the pure suspense story (what will happen), Millar noted that the two types normally blend in the crime story. (This synthesis is obvious in his novels, which work backward and forward in time.) Like all popular art forms, the suspense story "exists to be enjoyed," but its conventions also provide an artistic and social tradition: "It keeps the forms of the art alive for the writer to use. It trains his readers, endowing both writer and reader with a common vocabulary of structural shapes and narrative possibilities. It becomes a part of the language in which we think and feel, reaching our whole society and helping to hold our civilization together."[28] This eloquent pronouncement constituted Millar's valediction on his art. After one more novel he was silenced.

The Mystery Writers of America presented its Grand Master Award to Millar in 1974; yet he never won the best-novel Edgar. That year Millar shared his plans with Symons, who had become a trusted friend: "The book I'm working up now is last but one [in the Archer series] I think, though it could serve as the last if it had to, (I think). Really Archer hasn't hampered me much but it's time I essayed something new, with the option of returning to him later. The two books are already planned or semiplanned. . . . I hope I live long enough to write my own biography, as I have long intended to do. But not yet. There's still more living to be done, before I come full circle to my Pacific Coast beginnings."[29]

The Blue Hammer (1976) was a comeback novel. Millar had wanted to write it for a long time. Fourteen years elapsed between the first notebook entry and completion: "Every three or four years, I would do some work on it and I would ask myself, 'Should I go on with this?' Then I would put it away and do something else."[30] The eighteenth Archer novel is a summation of now familiar Millar themes and structures: questing youth, concealed paternity, assumed identities, hidden crimes—and the concatenations of past and present, money and sex. The title refers to arterial blood, and Millar took the phrase from a poem by Henri Coulette. His rejected titles included "Portrait of an Artist," "The Noon of Night," "Guilty Knowledge," and "The Silent Hammer."*

---

* John D. MacDonald complained to Knopf about the title, claiming that it infringed on his use of colors for the titles of his Travis McGee series.

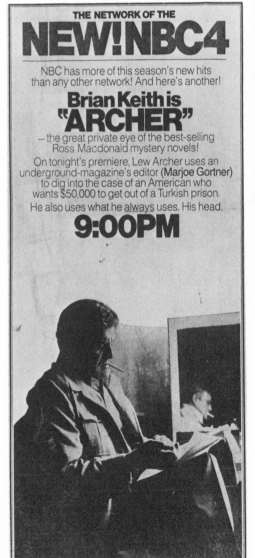

*Kenneth Millar accepting his Edgar from the
Mystery Writers of America, 3 May 1974*
(photograph © 1983 by Jill Krementz)

The New York Times, *30 January 1975*

Millar's notebooks reveal that the novel about the painter Richard Chantry, who went into hiding at the peak of his career, was an amalgam of several plot ideas. After planning an incest novel set in Canada, Millar queried himself: "CAN THIS BE COMBINED WITH THE CHANTRY CASE? WHY NOT? CHANTRY AND HIS 'WIFE' ARE BROTHER & SISTER AND HE'S IN HIDING FROM THE KILLING OF HER HUSBAND AND HAS TAKEN HIS IDENTITY."[31]

As finally evolved in *The Blue Hammer*, Chantry is actually William Mead, who murdered his putative half brother Richard Chantry and assumed his identity. Mead then killed Gerard Johnson and assumed his identity. For twenty-five years Mead/Chantry/Johnson has been hiding in Santa Teresa until his compulsion to paint exposes him and triggers two more murders. The web of hidden relationships was Millar's most intricate since *The Instant Enemy* and *The Goodbye Look*. But by this time Millar's serious readers had become trained to anticipate his plot reversals, thereby diluting the impact of the delayed revelations. When the reader learns that Richard Chantry's half brother William Mead was murdered, he begins to solve the plot for himself—which converts the literary experience into a guessing game. This process was not the result of a diminution of Millar's art or a shift in his intentions. Rather, it was the inevitable concomitant of his exploration of ritualized themes, which had become archetypal myths. Nonetheless, the critics' complaints about Millar's "formula" work were unjustified. He had not put old characters through their old paces. *The Blue Hammer* was an independently imagined work—with old ghosts.

Millar said that he made this novel a little more mellow and more tolerant than his previous work. Archer—who is in his sixties according to the chronology of the books, but admits to fifty in *The Blue Hammer*—has become introspective and confiding. He shares portentous comments about his work with the reader:

> I was growing weary of other people's pain and wondered if a black suit and a white collar might serve as armor against it.[32]

> Perhaps, after all, the truth I was looking for couldn't be found in the world. You had to go up on a mountain and wait for it, or find it in yourself.[33]

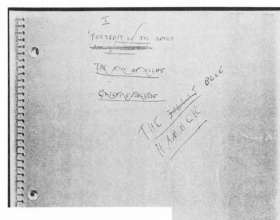

Notebook cover for The Blue Hammer
(Special Collections, University Library,
University of California, Irvine)

Working draft for The Blue Hammer
(Special Collections, University Library,
University of California, Irvine)

NOTEBOOK
49¢

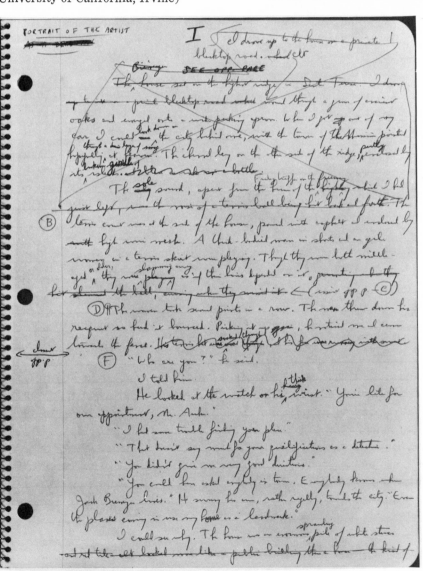

My chosen study was other men, hunted men in rented rooms, aging boys clutching at manhood before night fell and they grew suddenly old. If you were the therapist, how could you need therapy? If you were the hunter, you couldn't be hunted. Or could you?[34]

In fact, the deeper you go into a series of crimes, or any set of circumstances involving people who know each other, the more connectedness you find.[35]

These facts coming together in my mind gave me a kind of subterranean jolt, like an earth quake fault beginning to make its first tentative move.[36]

I felt for a moment that some ancient story was being repeated, that we had all been here before. I couldn't remember exactly what the story was or how it ended. But I felt that the ending somehow depended on me.[37]

The Blue Hammer allows Archer to discharge a piece of his own guilt going back to *The Moving Target* (1949). After preventing a murder accomplice from jumping off a pier, he confides to the reader:

As I marched Rico back to my car and got him safely inside of it, I understood one source of my satisfaction. Twenty-odd years ago, near an oil-stained pier like this, I had fought in the water a man named Puddler and drowned him.

Rico, whatever his sins, had served as an equalizer for one of mine.[38]

The tired and lonely Archer engages in his first love affair in *The Blue Hammer*. Though he has had intercourse with three other women in the series, his encounter with Betty Jo Siddon is the only time he commits himself: "I told her a story that I remembered from childhood. There had been a time, it said, when men and women were closer than twins and shared the same mortal body. I told her that when the two of us came together in my motel room, I felt that close to her. And when she dropped out of sight, I felt the loss of part of myself."³⁹ Betty Jo is an ambitious journalist and considerably younger than Archer. The novel ends with no promise of a lasting relationship.

Although it didn't hit the best seller list, "The New Lew Archer Novel" sold well. There were three Knopf trade printings; it was a Mystery Guild selection and a Literary Guild Featured Alternate. In England it was selected by both the Book Club Associates and the Thriller Book Club. Michael Wood in the *New York Times Book Review* judged it Millar's best work in recent years, but noted an "excess of self-consciousness."⁴⁰ Other reviewers indicated that Millar as well as Archer had gotten tired. Anatole Broyard, the reviewer for the daily *New York Times*, charged that the characters were at the mercy of the plot: "Here again is the arbitrariness and freedom of the fairy tale. Here is a prelogical world in which the grinding of fate's wheels is wholly unpredictable."⁴¹ The point is well taken, though not necessarily damaging. Millar had been writing fairy tales with unhappy endings for a long time. As Vladimir Nabokov insisted, "The truth is that great novels are great fairy tales. . . ."⁴²

In William Campbell Gault's dedication copy of *The Blue Hammer*, Millar wrote: "Who knows that writing well is the best revenge." Revenge for decay and death. After the completion of his twenty-fourth novel, Millar began to experience memory lapses and temporary confusion, which became more frequent. By 1981 his malady was diagnosed as Alzheimer's disease, irreversible presenile dementia. There were rumors about Millar's condition in the book world; and in 1982 Margaret Millar (who was going blind) discussed their plight in a *Los Angeles Times* interview:

"I said, 'Have you noticed how much friskier the dogs are in the morning?' He listened to me, nodded, then looked up and said, 'Yes, Currier and Ives did some of the best painting as young men.' . . . Mostly we have these long, silent nights now. I never leave him."⁴³

In 1976 Millar surprised an interviewer by naming Proust as his favorite writer. "He's really the one that seems to me to be the most complete of all novelists. The one who does everything and does it well, including the background of the war."⁴⁴ This choice should not have come

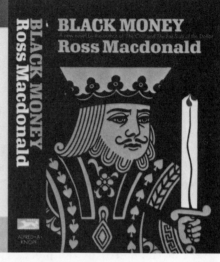

Ross Macdonald was born near San Francisco in 1915. He was educated in Canadian schools, traveled widely in Europe, and acquired advanced degrees and a Phi Beta Kappa key at the University of Michigan. In 1938 he married a Canadian girl who is now well known as the novelist Margaret Millar. Mr. Macdonald (Kenneth Millar in private life) taught school and later college, and served as Communications Officer aboard an escort carrier in the Pacific. For the past twenty years he has lived in Santa Barbara and has written mystery novels about the explosively changing society of his native state. His main interests, outside of literature, are conservation and politics. He is the current president of Mystery Writers of America. In 1964 his novel *The Chill* was given a Silver Dagger award by the Crime Writers' Association of Great Britain.

THE FAR SIDE OF THE DOLLAR (1965)

"Without in the least abating my admiration for Dashiell Hammett and Raymond Chandler, I should like to venture the heretical suggestion that Ross Macdonald is a better novelist than either of them."

ANTHONY BOUCHER, *The New York Times Book Review*

"Ross Macdonald is an important American novelist."

WILLIAM HOGAN, *San Francisco Chronicle*

THE CHILL (1964)

"The finest of Mr. Macdonald's prestige works."

DOROTHY B. HUGHES, New York *Herald Tribune*

"Macdonald should not be limited in audience to connoisseurs of mystery fiction. He is one of a handful of writers in the genre whose worth and quality surpass the limitations of the form."

ROBERT KIRSCH, *Los Angeles Times*

"Ross MacDonald in recent years has become the best writer we have about California and one of the country's best novelists."

ROGER SALE, *Argus*

Alfred A. Knopf, Publisher, New York

BLACK MONEY
Ross Macdonald

BLACK MONEY
A new novel by the author of *The Chill* and *The Far Side of the Dollar*
Ross Macdonald

ALFRED·A·
KNOPF

Ross Macdonald's famous detective, Lew Archer, is the kind you can drop a secret into and never it hit bottom. In his thirteenth strangest case he explores the sec of a rich California residentia munity. A beautiful young wo jilted her fiancé and taken up mysterious character who repres self as a French political refugee to investigate this man, Archer involved in several murders and tic swindle. Running through as a central theme in this mora bathing novel, is the corrupting in of the underworld and its money society.

Black Money is the most of the brilliant series of nove have won Ross Macdonald intern recognition.

Jacket design by Adelson & Eich

Ross Macdonald was born near San Francisco in 1915. He was educated in Canadian schools, traveled widely in Europe, and acquired advanced degrees and a Phi Beta Kappa key at the University of Michigan. In 1938 he married a Canadian girl who is now well known as the novelist Margaret Millar. Mr. Macdonald (Kenneth Millar in private life) taught school and later college, and served as Communications Officer aboard an escort carrier in the Pacific. For the past sixteen years he has lived in Santa Barbara and written mystery novels about the explosively changing society of his native state. His hobbies include sailing, tower diving, all-year swimming, and literary criticism.

What the reviewers said about
Ross Macdonald's last two books

THE WYCHERLY WOMAN

"Mr. Macdonald's prose is crisp, pungent and exemplary and so are his sensibilities. First-rate." —*New York Herald Tribune*

"This is not only a powerful suspense story, it is an exciting novel, brilliantly planned and skillfully written." —*St. Louis Post-Dispatch*

"You not only can read [Macdonald's mysteries] a second time, you should; that's when you'll truly notice all the intricate ironies, paradoxes, and poetic leitmotifs of which they are built." —*The New York Post*

"Ross MacDonald is one of the best living writers of the whodunit thriller, with not one spare ounce of flesh on the crackling dialogue. It's the kind of style and story that has a Bogart twist to its mouth." —*The Bookman*

THE FERGUSON AFFAIR

"A marvel of plotting....A disturbing novel of human beings and their tormented and tormenting relationships." —ANTHONY BOUCHER, *The New York Times*

"Macdonald's characterizations are skillful, his writing style is literate, and his plot...is varied and exciting. The result is a 'winner.'" —*New Orleans Times Picayune*

"Provocative characterizations and polished writing make it top-drawer suspense fare." —*Des Moines Register*

Alfred A. Knopf, Publisher   NEW YORK

the zebra-striped hearse | ROSS MACDONALD

the zebra-striped hearse

a new, powerful and fast-paced novel by the author of
THE WYCHERLY WOMAN and THE FERGUSON AFFAIR

ROSS MACDONALD

ALFRED A.
KNOPF

the zebra-strip hearse

HARRIET was a big girl, twenty-fi next birthday, but her father, Colin well, persisted in treating her as a When she came back from Mexic man she planned to marry, the Co sumed this match could not be Burke Damis, the prospective bri claimed to be a serious painter. H sidered him a genius, but nobody ever heard of him. So the Col Archer to look into Damis's backg most at once he discovered the b man stabbed to death with an scep while Damis and Harriet had drop sight.

The story moves with grace and steadily mounting excitement acros of California and through its soci Los Angeles to the Bay area, from ican colony on Mexico's Lake Chap floating population of gamblers girls on the south shore of Lake

This is Mr. Macdonald's tenth b the physical and moral adventure Archer, and perhaps the most fasc a brilliantly sustained, and widely a series. Like Raymond Chandler and Hammett before him, Ross Macdona for the general literate public. The fans also like his work is all to the

JACKET DESIGN BY PAUL BACON

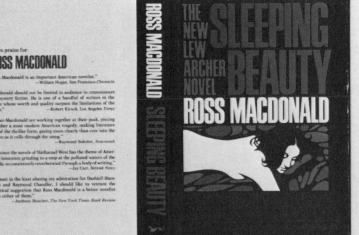

MACDONALD was born near [...]cisco in 1925. He was educated in Ca[...]schools, traveled widely in Europe, and [...] advanced degrees and a Phi Beta Kappa [...] University of Michigan. In 1938 he mar[...]anadian who is now well known as the [...]Margaret Millar. Mr. Macdonald (Kenneth [...] private life) taught school and later col[...]served as communications officer aboard [...] carrier in the Pacific. For over twenty [...] has lived in Santa Barbara and written [...] novels about the fascinating and changing [...] of his native state. Among his leading cr[...] in conservation and politics. He is a past [...] of the Mystery Writers of America. In [...] named *The Chill* was given a Silver Dagger [...] the Crime Writers' Association of Great [...] Mr. Macdonald's *The Far Side of the* [...] was named the best crime novel of 1965 by [...] organization. *The Moving Target* was [...] to the highly successful movie *Harper* [...] and *The Goodbye Look* (1969) and *The* [...] *und Man* (1971) were both national best [...]

[...] Knopf, Publisher, New York

More praise for
ROSS MACDONALD

"Ross Macdonald is an important American novelist."
—William Hogan, San Francisco Chronicle

"Macdonald should not be limited in audience to connoisseurs of mystery fiction. He is one of a handful of writers in the genre whose worth and quality surpass the limitations of the form."
—Robert Kirsch, Los Angeles Times

"Archer-Macdonald are working together at their peak, piecing together a most modern American tragedy, making literature out of the thriller form, gazing more clearly than ever into the future as it rolls through the smog."
—Raymond Sokolov, Newsweek

"Not since the novels of Nathanael West has the theme of American innocence grinding to a stop at the polluted waters of the Pacific so consistently reverberated through a body of writing."
—Jay Carr, Detroit News

"Without in the least abating my admiration for Dashiell Hammett and Raymond Chandler, I should like to venture the heretical suggestion that Ross Macdonald is a better novelist than either of them."
—Anthony Boucher, The New York Times Book Review

394-48474-6

$5.95

ROSS MACDONALD

THE NEW LEW ARCHER NOVEL

SLEEPING BEAUTY

ROSS MACDONALD

SLEEPING BEAUTY

KNOPF

The New York Times Book Review has called the novels of Ross Macdonald "the finest series of detective novels ever written by an American." And Eudora Welty says of his detective hero, Lew Archer: "He is of today, one of ours."

Ross Macdonald's new Lew Archer novel—his first since his best-selling and brilliantly acclaimed *The Underground Man* and *The Goodbye Look*—is itself strikingly "of today," of this moment in America. *Sleeping Beauty* plunges Archer into a fascinating and intricate case connected to a disastrous oil spill on the coast of Southern California. It involves him with three generations of the imposing Lennox family: whose offshore oil platform has caused the spill; whose young heiress, glimpsed for a haunting moment on the beach—handsome, angry-eyed, clutching an oil-drenched sea bird in her arms—has disappeared.

On her trail, Archer finds himself journeying into a horrendous past, into the hidden lives of a family twisted by money, by power, by a ruthless, almost compulsive instinct for infidelity—infidelity between husbands and wives, parents and children, infidelity to friends, dependents, duty and, in a sense, to the earth itself. As Archer moves among these people, among their lies and contradictions; as episodes distant in time are linked—a derelict stranger found dead, a ship destroyed by fire in World War II, a secret case of extortion, a child's long-ago glimpse of violence; as the novel moves to its climactic and complex resolution, the reader is once more held fast by the unique art of Ross Macdonald: crackling suspense rooted in strong perception of reality.

Jacket design by Hal Siegel

os Macdonald

[...]enneth Miller—was born in California [...] of Canadian-American ancestry. He [...]cated in Canada, and in 1938 mar[...] Canadian girl who is now well known [...]novelist under her married name, [...]et Millar. After several years of high[...]teaching, he was given a fellowship [...] University of Michigan, and took his [...]ate there with a study of Coleridge's [...]logy. He entered the Navy in 1944 [...]ved as a communications officer on [...]ort carrier. For some years he wrote [...] novels under the name John Ross [...]ald, but in 1956, for fear of possible [...]on with John D. Macdonald, changed [...] name to Ross Macdonald. He is a [...] Director of the Mystery Writers of [...] *The Ferguson Affair* is his fifteenth [...]ed book

[...]ED IN U.S.A.

What the reviewers said
about Ross Macdonald's last book
THE GALTON CASE

"Cumulatively exciting, beautifully plotted and written with taste, perception and compassion."
ANTHONY BOUCHER, The New York Times

"There has been a singularly involving excitement about Ross Macdonald's recent novels that is difficult to describe save by saying that the last page leads one back to the first all over again."
JAMES SANDOE, New York Herald Tribune

"A model of intelligently engineered excitement." The New Yorker

"A beautifully plotted mystery . . . This is one of the best."
Hartford Times

"A writer to whom superlatives cannot really do justice. . . . Do yourself a favor and get his book. See what can be done with a mystery novel."
Sacramento Bee

"This is an intricately wrought mystery-suspense story with a series of astonishing developments and a climax which tops them all. It'll keep you on the edge of your chair and finally knock you off it."
Columbus (Ohio) Citizen

"The story is laid out with a neat combination of intricacy and clarity. First class."
Washington News

Alfred·A·Knopf   Publisher   New York

THE FERGUSON AFFAIR

Ross Macdonald

THE FERGUSON AFFAIR

Ross Macdonald

A new and compelling mystery by the author of THE GALTON CASE and THE DOOMSTERS

ALFRED·A·KNOPF

AMBULANCE

$3.95

The Ferguson Affair
by Ross Macdonald

For his new novel Ross Macdonald has given us an explosive and fascinating mystery well up to the high standards he has established for himself and which few other writers of this genre can attain. In this novel his hero is Bill Gunnarson, young California lawyer, who takes the case of a nurse accused of theft—once the pockets of his very pregnant wife, who doesn't want him endangered.

But Bill's burning streak of justice prevail, and the thievery case embarks him on a trail that leads to a movie star of dubious reputation, a policeman of very strange behavior indeed, and a furious millionaire. Along with these there are scores and characters from every facet of contemporary California life: from the country club set to the fascinating Mexican-American world. And the trail is deeply interwoven with violence.

As always with Macdonald, this mystery reads like a novel of quality. His characters are real people, and they live in a society about which the author makes penetrating comments as the story races along.

Jacket design by Muni Giminez

Kenneth Millar at work, with Rollie (photograph © 1983 by Jill Krementz)

as a revelation. Millar, as well as his characters, had engaged in a search for lost time. In the end he was marooned in the present.

Kenneth Millar died in Santa Barbara on 11 July 1983—in his sixty-seventh year. As he had planned, his ashes were scattered "in the Santa Barbara Channel where, in the destructive element immersed, I have spent the best hours of my best days."[45]

APPENDIX
NOTES
BIBLIOGRAPHY
INDEX

APPENDIX

THE INWARD EYE: A REVALUATION
OF COLERIDGE'S PSYCHOLOGICAL CRITICISM

(Publication No. 3533)
Kenneth Millar, Ph.D.
University of Michigan, 1952*

The purpose of this study is to establish the meaning of Coleridge's literary criticism, by discovering its basic principles and method, and the historical purposes which it served. Since Coleridge based his poetic theory on psychological principles which he developed through observation and introspection, and through extensive reading in classical psychology beginning with Aristotle, a large part of the present study is devoted to his psychology, and to its background in European and English philosophy and psychology. Its immediate historical context was the dualistic philosophy of the seventeenth century and the mechanistic psychology which issued from it in the eighteenth century. Coleridge's own dynamic psychology, and the poetic which he developed *pari passu* with it, is explained as a conscious reaction against the 'passive mind' of associationism, and the divided mind of Cartesianism.

As the Introduction attempts to show, the dualistic philosophy and the mechanical psychology which dominated English thought throughout the eighteenth century were regarded by the early Romantic poets as threats to the unity

* *Dissertation Abstracts*, 12 (Ann Arbor, Mich.: University Microfilms, 1952).

and creativity of the human mind, on which the writing of poetry seemed to depend. Coleridge assumed the task of devising a dynamic psychology which should both explain and justify free poetic creation in an era of scientism. Chapter II describes his use of Aristotle for this purpose, and his completion of the classic theory of imitation with a conception of creative imagination, exempt from the necessity of telling scientific truth. This conception of creative mind arose, as Chapters III and IV demonstrate, from the dynamic theory of cognition and aesthetic expression which constituted Coleridge's answer to the eighteenth-century machine psychologies, exemplified by Hartley, and from the principle of psychic and natural unity which he opposed to Cartesian and Hobbesian dualistic philosophies described in Chapter V. In clearing the ground for a dynamic poetic, as Chapter VI shows, Coleridge made use of Berkeley's criticism of Locke; and was assisted in the formulation of his own imaginative poetic by the psychological school of eighteenth-century critics which stemmed from Addison.

The concluding chapters, VII and VIII, describe in detail the theories of symbolic expression and poetic method which Coleridge based on his psychology, and his closely related theories of organic unity, poetic belief, and poetic value. In interpreting these theories in the light of a psychology which provided Coleridge with his critical principles, the present study aims to present a more coherent and exact exposition of their meaning than has previously been available, and to show that they constitute the central statement of the English Romantic movement.

NOTES

INTRODUCTION
1. W. H. Auden, "The Guilty Vicarage: Notes on the Detective Story, by an Addict," *Harper's Magazine*, May 1948, pp. 406–412.

ONE
1. Kenneth Millar, "The Yellow Dusters," (Toronto) *Saturday Night*, 11 November 1939, p. 24.
2. Ross Macdonald, "A Preface to *The Galton Case*," in *Afterwords: Novelists on Their Novels*, ed. Thomas McCormack (New York: Harper & Row, 1968), pp. 146–159. Collected as "Writing *The Galton Case*," in Ross Macdonald, *Self-Portrait*, ed. Ralph B. Sipper (Santa Barbara: Capra Press, 1981), p. 51.
3. John Millar, "Oor Kennie," *Los Gatos Mail*, 16 December 1915, p. 8.
4. Jerry Tutunjian, "A Conversation with Ross Macdonald," *Tamarack Review* 62 (1974): 68.
5. Ross Macdonald, "Foreword" to *Archer in Jeopardy* (New York: Knopf, 1979), pp. v–vi. Also in Macdonald, *Self-Portrait*, p. 16.

6. Macdonald, "Writing *The Galton Case*," in *Self-Portrait*, p. 52.

7. Brad Darrach, "Ross Macdonald: The Man Behind the Mysteries," *People*, 8 July 1974, p. 29.

8. Robert A. Wright, "Broad Spectrum of Writers Attacks Obscenity Rulings," *New York Times*, 21 August 1973, p. 38.

9. "The Books That Made Writers," *New York Times Book Review*, 25 November 1979, p. 84.

10. Ross Macdonald, "Down These Streets a Mean Man Must Go," *Antaeus* 25–26 (Spring/Summer 1977): 211–216. Also in Macdonald, *Self-Portrait*, p. 7.

11. Dick Adler, "Will the Real Ross Macdonald Please Keep Writing?" *Los Angeles Times West*, 10 December 1967, p. 82.

12. Robert Easton to MJB (Matthew J. Bruccoli), 22 September 1982.

13. Ken Miller. "The South Sea Soup Co.," *The Grumbler* (1931), pp. 23–25.

14. Macdonald, "Foreword" to *Archer in Jeopardy*, p. vi. Also in Macdonald, *Self-Portrait*, p. 16.

15. Ed Wilcox, "The Secret Success of Kenneth Millar," *New York Sunday News*, 21 November 1971, p. 158.

16. Robert Easton to MJB, 22 September 1982.

17. Ibid.

18. Kenneth Millar to Julian Symons, 20 January 1973.

19. "A Conversation with the Author," *Santa Barbara News & Review*, 23 March 1973, p. 7.

20. Kenneth Millar, "Introduction," in Matthew J. Bruccoli, *Kenneth Millar/Ross Macdonald: A Checklist* (Detroit: Gale Research/Bruccoli Clark, 1971), p. xiii. Also in Macdonald, *Self-Portrait*, p. 25.

21. Jerry Speir, *Ross Macdonald* (New York: Ungar, 1978), p. 7.

22. Kenneth Millar to Julian Symons, 20 January 1973.

23. Gene Davidson and John Knoerle, "Ross Macdonald Interview," *Mystery*, November/December 1979, p. 8.

24. Isaac Anderson, "The Crime Corner," *New York Times Book Review*, 1 October 1944, p. 12.

25. Kenneth Millar, *The Dark Tunnel* (New York: Dodd, Mead, 1944), p. 22.

26. Davidson and Knoerle, "Ross Macdonald Interview," p. 8.

27. Kenneth Millar, "Find the Woman," in *Maiden Murders* (New York: Harper, 1952), pp. 97–98.

28. Ibid.

29. Millar, "Introduction" to *Kenneth Millar/Ross Macdonald: A Checklist*, p. xiv. Also in Macdonald, *Self-Portrait*, p. 26.

30. Clifford A. Ridley, "Yes, Most of My Chronicles Are Chronicles of Misfortune," *National Observer*, 31 July 1976, p. 17.

31. Kenneth Millar, *Blue City* (New York: Knopf, 1947), p. 163.
32. Ross Macdonald, "In The First Person," in *Self-Portrait*, p. 41.
33. Kenneth Millar to Ashbel Green, 29 May 1972. University of California, Irvine.
34. *Blue City*, p. 276.
35. Will Cuppy, "Mystery and Adventure," *New York Herald Tribune Weekly Book Review*, 24 August 1974, p. 10.
36. "Mystery and Crime," *New Yorker*, 23 August 1947, p. 80.
37. Kenneth Millar, *The Three Roads* (New York: Knopf, 1948), p. 20.
38. Helen B. Parker, "Companions for Vacation Hammocks," *New York Times*, 25 July 1948, p. 15.
39. 13 June 1969. Knopf Papers. Humanities Research Center, University of Texas.
40. Ross Macdonald, "Foreword" to *Archer in Hollywood* (New York: Knopf, 1967), p. vii. Also in Macdonald, *Self-Portrait*, p. 35.
41. Millar, "Introduction" to *Kenneth Millar/Ross Macdonald: A Checklist*, p. xv. Also in Macdonald, *Self-Portrait*, p. 26.

TWO
1. Macdonald, "Foreword" to *Archer in Hollywood*, p. vii. Also in Macdonald, *Self-Portrait*, p. 35.
2. 10 August 1948. Knopf Papers. Humanities Research Center, University of Texas.
3. Alfred A. Knopf to Kenneth Millar, 2 September 1948. Knopf Papers. Humanities Research Center, University of Texas.
4. Kenneth Millar to Ivan von Auw, 4 September 1948. Copy. Humanities Research Center, University of Texas.
5. Kenneth Millar to Ivan von Auw, 12 September 1948. Copy. Humanities Research Center, University of Texas.
6. Kenneth Millar to Blanche Knopf, 24 October 1948. Knopf Papers. Humanities Research Center, University of Texas.
7. John Macdonald, *The Morning Target* (New York: Knopf, 1949), p. 109.
8. Raymond F. Jones, "A New Raymond Chandler?" *Los Angeles Magazine*, March 1963, p. 58.
9. Ross Macdonald, "The Writer as Detective Hero," *Show*, January 1965, pp. 34–36. Also in Macdonald, *Self-Portrait*, p. 121.
10. Robert Easton to MJB, 22 September 1982.
11. Macdonald, "The Writer as Detective Hero," in *Self-Portrait*, p. 113.
12. Macdonald, "Down These Streets a Mean Man Must Go," in *Self-Portrait*, p. 7.
13. Wilcox, "The Secret Success of Kenneth Millar," p. 159.

14. Kenneth Millar to Ivan von Auw, 4 September 1948. Copy. Humanities Research Center, University of Texas.

15. Matthew J. Bruccoli and Jennifer Atkinson, eds., *As Ever, Scott Fitz—* (Philadelphia and New York: Lippincott, 1972), p. 357.

16. "Morris—The Territory Ahead Is Always Behind Us," *San Francisco Chronicle*, 28 December 1958, p. 15.

17. Macdonald, "Foreword" to *Archer in Hollywood*, p. viii. Also in *Self-Portrait*, p. 36.

18. Martha MacGregor, "The Week in Books," *New York Post*, 9 May 1965, p. 49.

19. Macdonald, "In The First Person," in *Self-Portrait*, p. 44.

20. Lawrence Treat, ed., *Mystery Writer's Handbook* (Cincinnati: Writer's Digest, 1976), p. 264.

21. Ralph B. Sipper, "An Interview with Ross Macdonald," in Macdonald, *Self-Portrait*, p. 92.

22. Anthony Boucher, "Criminals at Large," *New York Times Book Review*, 3 April 1949, p. 28.

23. Frank MacShane, ed., *The Letters of Raymond Chandler* (New York: Columbia University Press, 1982), pp. 163–164.

24. Macdonald, "The Writer as Detective Hero," *Show*, January 1965, p. 36. Millar revised this statement for *On Crime Writing* (Santa Barbara: Capra Press, 1973): "My narrator Archer's wider and less rigidly stylized range of expression, at least in more recent novels, is related to a central difference between him and Marlowe. Marlowe's voice is limited by his role as the hardboiled hero" (p. 22).

25. John Ross Macdonald, *The Drowning Pool* (New York: Knopf, 1950), p. 166.

26. Macdonald, "In the First Person," in *Self-Portrait*, p. 41.

27. Kenneth Millar to MJB, n.d. [1971].

28. "Introduction" to *Kenneth Millar/Ross Macdonald: A Checklist*, p. xvi. Also in Macdonald, *Self-Portrait*, p. 27.

29. Kenneth Millar, "The Inward Eye: A Revaluation of Coleridge's Psychological Criticism." Unpublished doctoral dissertation, University of Michigan, 1952, p. 2.

30. Millar, "The Inward Eye," p. 434.

31. Robert Easton to MJB, 22 September 1982.

32. Herbert Harker to MJB, 24 October 1982.

33. Ralph Sipper, "Faces of Ross Macdonald," *Santa Barbara Magazine*, Winter 1980, p. 68.

34. Ross Macdonald, "Goldenrod," *New York Times Book Review*, 11 June 1972, p. 6.

35. Herbert Harker to MJB, 24 October 1982.

36. Kenneth Millar to Alfred A. Knopf, 20 February 1950. Knopf Papers. Humanities Research Center, University of Texas.

37. Ibid.

38. Trevor Meldal-Johnsen, "Ross Macdonald," *Gallery*, March 1976, p. 85.

39. Anthony Boucher, "Criminals at Large," *New York Times Book Review*, 5 August 1951, p. 17.

40. Kenneth Millar to Anthony Boucher, 9 July [1951]. Lilly Library, Indiana University.

41. Kenneth Millar to David Herrmann, 20 September 1951. Humanities Research Center, University of Texas.

42. James Sandoe, "Mystery and Suspense," *New York Herald Tribune*, 4 May 1952, p. 11.

43. *London Times Literary Supplement*, 20 November 1953, p. 737.

44. Macdonald, "In the First Person," in *Self-Portrait*, p. 43.

45. Kenneth Millar to Anthony Boucher, 3 May 1953. Lilly Library, Indiana University.

46. Alfred A. Knopf to Kenneth Millar, 21 August 1952. Knopf Papers. Humanities Research Center, University of Texas.

47. Kenneth Millar to Alfred A. Knopf, 28 August 1952. Knopf Papers. Humanities Research Center, University of Texas.

48. Kenneth Millar to Alfred A. Knopf, 2 November 1953. Knopf Papers. Humanities Research Center, University of Texas.

49. Anthony Boucher, "Criminals at Large," *New York Times Book Review*, 1 August 1954, p. 15.

50. Kenneth Millar to Anthony Boucher, 9 August 1954. Lilly Library, Indiana University.

51. "Reasonable Facsimile," *Time*, 26 July 1954, p. 82.

52. Ross Macdonald, *The Barbarous Coast* (New York: Knopf, 1956), p. 119.

53. Kenneth Millar to Ivan von Auw, 13 January 1956. Princeton University Library.

54. "Probation Granted to Hit-Run Driver," *Santa Barbara News-Press*, 27 August 1956, pp. A1–2.

55. Kenneth Millar to Ivan von Auw, 11 May 1956. Princeton University Library.

56. Macdonald, "Foreword" to *Archer at Large* (New York: Knopf, 1970), p. viii. Also in *Self-Portrait*, p. 30.

57. "Philip Oaks Meets a Best-seller Who is IN FOR LIFE," *London Sunday Times*, 24 October 1971, p. 33.

58. Kenneth Millar to Ivan von Auw, 27 May 1957. Princeton University Library.

59. Kenneth Millar to Alfred A. Knopf, 9 March 1958. Knopf Papers. Humanities Research Center, University of Texas.

60. Ross Macdonald, *The Doomsters* (New York: Knopf, 1958), p. 222.
61. Macdonald, "The Writer as Detective Hero," in *Self-Portrait*, p. 120.
62. Ridley, "Yes, Most of My Chronicles Are Chronicles of Misfortune," p. 17.
63. *The Doomsters*, p. 250.
64. Peter Preston, "The Further Side of the Dollar," *Manchester Guardian*, 23 October 1971, p. 9.
65. *The Doomsters*, p. 238.
66. *The Doomsters*, p. 250.
67. *The Doomsters*, pp. 237–238.
68. Kenneth Millar to Alfred A. Knopf, 9 March 1958. Knopf Papers. Humanities Research Center, University of Texas.
69. Kenneth Millar to Dorothy Olding, 27 May 1957. Princeton University Library.
70. Kenneth Millar to Dorothy Olding, 21 June 1957. Princeton University Library.
71. Kenneth Millar to Ivan von Auw, 26 August 1957. Princeton University Library.
72. Ross Macdonald, "Research into the History of Detective Fiction," *San Francisco Chronicle—This World*, 15 February 1959, p. 29. Appears in Macdonald, *A Collection of Reviews* (Northridge, Calif.: Lord John Press, 1979), pp. 1–4.
73. Ross Macdonald, "Leacock Loved and Ornamented the Anglo-Canadian Language," *San Francisco Chronicle—This World*, 3 January 1960, p. 21. Appears in Macdonald, *A Collection of Reviews*, p. 65.

THREE

1. Raymond A. Sokolov, "The Art of Murder," *Newsweek*, 22 March 1971, p. 108.
2. Ridley, "Yes, Most of My Chronicles Are Chronicles of Misfortune," p. 17.
3. Kenneth Millar to Alfred A. Knopf, 9 March 1958. Knopf Papers. Humanities Research Center, University of Texas.
4. Macdonald, collected as "Writing *The Galton Case*," in *Self-Portrait*, pp. 50–51.
5. Ibid., p. 54.
6. Facsimile, in Matthew J. Bruccoli, *Kenneth Millar/Ross Macdonald: A Checklist*, p. 61.
7. Macdonald, "Writing *The Galton Case*," in *Self-Portrait*, pp. 55–56.
8. Donald Davie to MJB, 14 August 1982.
9. Kenneth Millar to Julian Symons, 10 July 1973.
10. Macdonald, "Writing *The Galton Case*," in *Self-Portrait*, p. 56.
11. Ibid., pp. 57–58.
12. Ross Macdonald, *The Galton Case* (New York: Knopf, 1959), p. 3.
13. Tutunjian, "A Conversation with Ross Macdonald," p. 81.

14. Macdonald, "Writing *The Galton Case*," in *Self-Portrait*, p. 59.

15. Kenneth Millar to Alfred A. Knopf, 24 June 1958. Knopf Papers. Humanities Research Center, University of Texas.

16. Anthony Boucher, "Criminals at Large," *New York Times Book Review*, 29 March 1959, p. 20.

17. *London Times Literary Supplement*, 12 February 1960, p. 93.

18. Kenneth Millar to Steven R. Carter in Carter, "Ross Macdonald: The Complexity of the Modern Quest for Justice," *Mystery and Detection Annual*, 1973, p. 66.

19. Burt Prelutsky, "Big Fish in the Big Pond," *Los Angeles Times Calendar*, 25 November 1973, p. 18.

20. Ira Greenberg, "Mystery Writer Has Only One Clue: His Daughter's $10 Check," *New York Post*, 10 June 1959, p. 26; "Coed, Missing for 11 Days, Returns Home," *Los Angeles Times*, 12 June 1959, I, p. 16.

21. Macdonald, "The Writer as Detective Hero," in *Self-Portrait*, p. 120.

22. Carter, "Ross Macdonald: The Complexity of the Modern Quest for Justice," p. 77.

23. Ross Macdonald, *The Instant Enemy* (New York: Knopf, 1968), p. 122.

24. James Sandoe, "Mystery and Suspense," *New York Herald Tribune Lively Arts*, 25 June 1961, p. 37.

25. Ross Macdonald, ed., *Great Stories of Suspense* (New York: Knopf, 1974), p. xvi.

26. Ross Macdonald, *The Far Side of the Dollar* (New York: Knopf, 1965), p. 180.

27. *The Far Side of the Dollar*, p. 119.

28. Ridley, "Yes, Most of My Chronicles are Chronicles of Misfortune," p. 17.

29. George Grella, "Evil Plots," *New Republic*, 26 July 1975, pp. 24–26.

30. Anthony Boucher, "Criminals at Large," *New York Times Book Review*, (24 January 1965), p. 42.

31. Julian Symons, *London Sunday Times*, 19 September 1965, p. 49.

32. Ross Macdonald, *Mystery Writers' Annual*, 1965, p. 2.

33. Herbert Harker to MJB, 24 October 1982.

34. "A Conversation with the Author," *Santa Barbara News & Review*, 23 March 1973, p. 7.

35. Tutunjian, "A Conversation with Ross Macdonald," p. 76.

36. Ross Macdonald, *Black Money* (New York: Knopf, 1966), p. 230.

37. *The Instant Enemy*, p. 22.

38. *The Instant Enemy*, p. 45.

39. *The Instant Enemy*, p. 74.

40. *The Instant Enemy*, p. 77.

41. *The Instant Enemy*, p. 165.

42. Adler, "Will the Real Ross Macdonald Please Keep Writing?" p. 86.
43. Kenneth Millar to Ashbel Green, 28 September 1968. Humanities Research Center, University of Texas.

FOUR

1. Kenneth Millar to Ashbel Green, 28 September 1968. Humanities Research Center, University of Texas.
2. William Goldman, *New York Times Book Review*, 1 June 1969, p. 2.
3. John Leonard, "Ross Macdonald, His Lew Archer and Other Secret Selves," *New York Times Book Review*, 1 June 1969. p. 2.
4. "Summer Sleuthing," *Newsweek*, 28 July 1969, p. 80.
5. Ross Macdonald, *The Goodbye Look* (New York: Knopf, 1969), p. 127.
6. *The Goodbye Look*, p. 151.
7. *The Goodbye Look*, p. 232.
8. Ed Wilcox, "The Secret Success of Kenneth Millar," p. 159.
9. Robert Easton to MJB, 22 September 1982.
10. Kenneth Millar to Dorothy Olding, 8 November 1970. Princeton University Library.
11. Ross Macdonald, *The Underground Man* (New York: Knopf, 1971), p. 226.
12. *The Underground Man*, p. 31.
13. Kenneth Millar to Alfred A. Knopf, 23 January 1971. Knopf Papers. Humanities Research Center, University of Texas.
14. *The Underground Man*, p. 18.
15. *The Underground Man*, p. 96.
16. Kenneth Millar to Ashbel Green, 19 July 1970. University of California, Irvine.
17. Sokolov, "The Art of Murder," p. 108.
18. Eudora Welty, *New York Times Book Review*, 14 February 1971, p. 29.
19. Bruce Cook, "Ross Macdonald: The Prince in the Poorhouse," *New Catholic World*, October 1971, pp. 27–30.
20. Richard Schickel, "Detective Story," *Commentary*, September 1971, p. 98.
21. Macdonald, *Self-Portrait*, p. 124.
22. Ross Macdonald, "Introduction" to *Lew Archer Private Investigator*, pp. ix-x. Also in Macdonald, *Self-Portrait*, p. 18.
23. "Writers' Writers," *New York Times Book Review*, 4 December 1977, p. 62.
24. Kenneth Millar to Julian Symons, 19 January 1972.
25. Crawford Woods, *New York Times Book Review*, 20 May 1973, p. 55.
26. Ross Macdonald, *New York Times Book Review*, 5 August 1973, p. 24.
27. *New Republic*, 2 June 1973, p. 29.
28. Ross Macdonald, "Introduction" to *Great Stories of Suspense*, pp. xvi–xvii.

Notes

29. Kenneth Millar to Julian Symons, 10 September 1974.
30. Celeste Durant, "Ross Macdonald: After 19th Novel," *Chicago Sun Times Living*, 28 July 1976, pp. 69, 74.
31. Millar papers, University of California, Irvine.
32. Ross Macdonald, *The Blue Hammer* (New York: Knopf, 1976), p. 59.
33. *The Blue Hammer*, p. 117.
34. *The Blue Hammer*, pp. 122–123.
35. *The Blue Hammer*, p. 133.
36. *The Blue Hammer*, p. 153.
37. *The Blue Hammer*, p. 187.
38. *The Blue Hammer*, p. 176.
39. *The Blue Hammer*, p. 240.
40. Michael Wood, *New York Times Book Review*, 13 June 1976, p. 4.
41. Anatole Broyard, "Books of the Times," *New York Times*, 11 June 1976, p. C21.
42. Vladimir Nabokov, *Lectures on Literature* (New York and London: Harcourt Brace Jovanovich/Bruccoli Clark, 1980), p. 2.
43. Wayne Warga, "The Millars: Tale of Fortitude," *Los Angeles Times*, 11 February 1982, p. V-26.
44. Meldal-Johnsen, "Ross Macdonald," p. 90.
45. Kenneth Millar to Julian Symons, 6 March 1973.

BIBLIOGRAPHY

BOOKS

The Dark Tunnel (Kenneth Millar). New York: Dodd, Mead, 1944. Republished as
  I Die Slowly (New York: Lion, 1955).

Trouble Follows Me (Kenneth Millar). New York: Dodd, Mead, 1946. Republished
  as *Night Train* (New York: Lion, 1955).

Blue City (Kenneth Millar). New York: Knopf, 1947; London: Cassell, 1949.

The Three Roads (Kenneth Millar). New York: Knopf, 1948; London: Cassell,
  1950.

*The Moving Target (John Macdonald). New York: Knopf, 1949; London: Cassell,
  1951. Republished as *Harper* (New York: Pocket, 1966).

*The Drowning Pool (John Ross Macdonald). New York: Knopf, 1950; London:
  Cassell, 1952.

*The Way Some People Die (John Ross Macdonald). New York: Knopf, 1951;
  London: Cassell, 1953.

* Asterisks indicate Lew Archer novels.

The Ivory Grin (John Ross Macdonald). New York: Knopf, 1952; London: Cassell, 1953. Republished as *Marked for Murder* (New York: Pocket, 1953).

Meet Me at the Morgue (John Ross Macdonald). New York: Knopf, 1953; *Experience with Evil*. London: Cassell, 1954.

Find a Victim (John Ross Macdonald). New York: Knopf, 1954; London: Cassell, 1955.

The Name Is Archer (John Ross Macdonald). New York: Bantam, 1955; London: Fontana, 1976. "Find the Woman," "Gone Girl," "The Bearded Lady," "The Suicide," "Guilt-Edged Blonde," "The Sinister Habit," "Wild Goose Chase."

The Barbarous Coast (Ross Macdonald). New York: Knopf, 1956; London: Cassell, 1957.

The Doomsters. New York: Knopf, 1958; London: Cassell, 1958.

The Galton Case. New York: Knopf, 1959; London: Cassell, 1960.

The Ferguson Affair. New York: Knopf, 1960; London: Collins, 1961.

The Wycherly Woman. New York: Knopf, 1961; London: Collins, 1962.

The Zebra-Striped Hearse. New York: Knopf, 1962; London: Collins, 1963.

The Chill. New York: Knopf, 1964; London: Collins, 1964.

The Far Side of the Dollar. New York: Knopf, 1965; London: Collins, 1965.

Black Money. New York: Knopf, 1966; London: Collins, 1966.

The Instant Enemy. New York: Knopf, 1968; London: Collins, 1968.

The Goodbye Look. New York: Knopf, 1969; London: Collins, 1969.

The Underground Man. New York: Knopf, 1971; London: Collins, 1971.

Sleeping Beauty. New York: Knopf, 1973; London: Collins, 1973.

On Crime Writing. Santa Barbara: Capra Press, 1973. "The Writer as Detective Hero" and "Writing *The Galton Case*."

Great Stories of Suspense (editor). New York: Knopf, 1974.

The Blue Hammer. New York: Knopf, 1976; London: Collins, 1976.

Lew Archer, Private Investigator. New York: Mysterious Press, 1977. Adds two stories to *The Name Is Archer*: "Midnight Blue" and "The Sleeping Dog."

A Collection of Reviews. Northridge, Calif.: Lord John Press, 1979. Book reviews.

Self-Portrait. Edited by Ralph B. Sipper. Santa Barbara: Capra Press, 1981. Articles.

Early Millar. Santa Barbara: Cordelia Editions, 1982. Juvenilia by Kenneth and Margaret Millar.

COLLECTIONS

Archer in Hollywood. New York: Knopf, 1967. *The Moving Target, The Way Some People Die, The Barbarous Coast*.

Archer at Large. New York: Knopf, 1970. *The Galton Case, The Chill, Black Money*.

Archer in Jeopardy. New York: Knopf, 1979. *The Doomsters, The Zebra-Striped Hearse, The Instant Enemy*.

SELECTED ARTICLES FIRST APPEARING IN BOOKS

"A Preface to *The Galton Case*." In *Afterwords: Novelists on Their Novels*. Edited by Thomas McCormack. New York: Harper & Row, 1968.

"Introduction." In Matthew J. Bruccoli, *Kenneth Millar/Ross Macdonald: A Checklist*. Detroit: Gale Research/Bruccoli Clark, 1971.

"Introduction." In Robert Easton, *Black Tide*. New York: Delacorte Press, 1972.

SELECTED MAGAZINE AND NEWSPAPER APPEARANCES

"The South Sea Soup Co." (Ken Miller). *The Grumbler* (1931), pp. 23–25. Parody; first appearance in print.

"Fatal Facility" (Kenneth Millar). (Toronto) *Saturday Night*, 29 July 1939, p. 20. Poem; first professional publication.

"Find the Woman" (Kenneth Millar). *Ellery Queen's Mystery Magazine*, June 1946, pp. 102–119. Story.

"The Sky Hook" (Kenneth Millar). *American Mercury*, January 1948, pp. 74–79. Story.

"The Bearded Lady" (Kenneth Millar). *American Magazine*, October 1948, pp. 152–166. Story.

"Shock Treatment" (Kenneth Millar). *Manhunt*, January 1953, pp. 71–80. Story.

"The Imaginary Blonde" (Kenneth Millar). *Manhunt*, February 1953, pp. 1–27. Story; collected as "Gone Girl."

"The Guilty Ones" (John Ross Macdonald). *Manhunt*, May 1953, pp. 1–21. Story; collected as "The Sinister Habit."

"The Beat-Up Sister" (John Ross Macdonald). *Manhunt*, October 1953, pp. 110–140. Story; collected as "The Suicide."

"Guilt-Edged Blonde" (John Ross Macdonald). *Manhunt*, January 1954, pp. 1–12. Story.

"Wild Goose Chase" (John Ross Macdonald). *Ellery Queen's Mystery Magazine*, July 1954, pp. 123–141. Story.

"Midnight Blue" (Ross Macdonald). *Ed McBain's Mystery Magazine*, October 1960, pp. 2–24. Story.

"Homage to Dashiell Hammett" (Ross Macdonald). *Mystery Writers' Annual*, 1964, pp. 8, 24. Article.

"A Death Road for the Condor" (Ross Macdonald). *Sports Illustrated*, 6 April 1964, pp. 86–89. Article.

"The Writer as Detective Hero" (Ross Macdonald). *Show*, January 1965, pp. 34–36. Article.

"The Sleeping Dog" (Ross Macdonald). *Argosy*, April 1965, pp. 42–43, 90–95. Story.

"Murder in The Library" (Kenneth Millar). *Mystery Writers' Annual*, 1965, p. 2. Article.

"Cain × 3" (Ross Macdonald). *New York Times Book Review*, 2 March 1969, pp. 1, 49–51. Book review.

"Life with the Blob" (Ross Macdonald). *Sports Illustrated*, 21 April 1969, pp. 50–52, 57–60. Article.

"Santa Barbarans Cite an 11th Commandment: 'Thou Shalt Not Abuse the Earth'" (Ross Macdonald and Robert Easton). *New York Times Magazine*, 12 October 1969, pp. 32–33, 142–149, 151, 156. Article.

"Down These Streets a Mean Man Must Go" (Ross Macdonald). *Antaeus* 25–26 (Spring/Summer 1977): 211–216. Article.

"The Private Detective" (Ross Macdonald). *New York Times Book Review*, 23 October 1977, pp. 2, 40–41. Introduction to *Lew Archer, Private Investigator*.

SELECTED INTERVIEWS

Adler, Dick. "Will the Real Ross Macdonald Please Keep Writing?" *Los Angeles Times West*, 10 December 1967, pp. 79–80, 82–83, 85–86.

Bakerman, Jane S. "A Slightly Stylized Conversation with Ross Macdonald." *Writer's Yearbook* 52 (1981): 86, 88–89, 111.

Carroll, Jon. "Ross Macdonald in Raw California." *Esquire*, June 1972, pp. 148–149, 188.

Darrach, Brad. "Ross Macdonald: The Man Behind the Mysteries." *People*, 8 July 1974, pp. 26–30.

Grogg, Sam, Jr. "Ross Macdonald: At the Edge." *Journal of Popular Culture* 7 (Summer 1973): 213–222.

Leonard, John. "Ross Macdonald, His Lew Archer and Other Secret Selves." *New York Times Book Review*, 1 June 1969, pp. 2, 19.

Meldal-Johnsen, Trevor. "Ross Macdonald." *Gallery*, March 1976, pp. 84–88, 90.

Ridley, Clifford A. "Yes, Most of My Chronicles Are Chronicles of Misfortune." *National Observer*, 31 July 1976, p. 17.

Tutunjian, Jerry. "A Conversation with Ross Macdonald." *Tamarack Review* 62 (1974): 66–85.

Wilcox, Ed. "The Secret Success of Kenneth Millar." *New York Sunday News*, 21 November 1971, pp. 158–159.

SELECTED BOOKS AND ARTICLES ABOUT MACDONALD

Bruccoli, Matthew J. *Kenneth Millar/Ross Macdonald: A Descriptive Bibliography*. Pittsburgh: University of Pittsburgh Press, 1983.

Sokolov, Raymond A. "The Art of Murder." *Newsweek*, 22 March 1971, pp. 101–104, 106, 108.

Speir, Jerry. *Ross Macdonald*. New York: Ungar, 1978.

Wolfe, Peter. *Dreamers Who Live Their Dreams: The World of Ross Macdonald's Novels*. Bowling Green, Ohio: Bowling Green University Popular Press, 1976.

INDEX